A Curb Caste Experience

⌘

Michael McNaney

Edited By Alexandra Bodkins

ISBN-13: 978-1537410203
ISBN-10: 1537410202

CONTENTS

* References throughout this book are marked as (*#)

☺ - *Introduction*

Have you ever wanted to just get up and go? I mean just pick up and leave. Not necessarily to never come back again or to find another place to live, but have you ever said to yourself, "*Screw this, I'm soo tired of this, I'm sooo bored, what's next?*" I have, in fact I've had this feeling quite often in my life. As time rolls on, I've stopped many times to indulge this little mensch in my head and dropped everything to follow, but follow what? Most of the time, I have no idea of where I'll end up or what might happen along the way. I'll get this itch and soon be pointed in a totally new direction. Generally, all I will have for a plan is a very limited and easily obtainable goal, let the rest of the dice fall as they may, a sort of coddiwomple in reverse.

At first, when I was younger, it was a bit scary. More recently, I've learned to relish this feeling. Occasionally I'll sit and wonder when the next time this wave of whimsy will appear, or more importantly, when I'll have the funds to facilitate such a proposition.

This restless soul syndrome, this *affliction* as it were, is not unique to me. It is a common occurrence to many people of many cultures throughout the world and referred to in English as wanderlust. Although urging us forward to many wondrous places, unfortunately wanderlust is not free. Even to the lowliest of homeless vagabond, travel costs an occasional amount of coinage and effort to maintain an existence on the road.

In my youth, friends and I would hitchhike from one

end of the state to the other just to see a band, like Stevie Ray Vaughn's "Double Trouble," play in a small college auditorium.
In one instance, at sixteen years old, a friend of mine and I made up a story to tell our parents about how we were essentially going to stay at each others house for a week and go camping, etc. I was going to be at his house for a week or so and his parents thought he would be at my house for the same amount of time. Not an uncommon thing for children to do even today when school is out and everyone including the parents are bored. Back then this type of conspiracy was easier to pull off. Telephones were stationary, answering machines were optional and the community in general policed unruly or needful kids.
My friend and I had each grubbed and stolen a handful of bucks from our parents and caught a ride with a jealous friend as far as he was comfortable taking us. From there it was thumbs out till Miami. I started hitching long before this trip but this one in particular sticks with me because of its planned destination. It was a failed attempt to see one of my favorite bands at that time, Led Zeppelin.
We were on the road for two days and had even slept in the ditch one night of the pilgrimage before arriving in Jacksonville, Florida. There, we heard the news on a local Rock-n'-Roll radio station that John Bonham, Led Zeppelin's drummer, had died in Germany before the band's concert trip to the states. We were crushed of course but as was quite often the case, we met up with a few cool people and partied there in *J-ville* for a day

or so before heading back home. We then spent the last couple days actually doing what we told our parents we were going to do.
In those days, hitching rides was fast and easy. As kids we already walked everywhere we went and most likely covered several hundred miles per summer just getting from here to there, but hitching made things much easier and generally a lot more interesting. On foot and bicycle my range of roam was limited to a few miles until about twelve years old. I think the time two friends and I hitched our first failed ride from Rockford to Chicago to see a Cubs game is when everything changed. Failed or not, the realization came, this was freedom. I hitched so much as a teenager and have so many stories and adventures in my head, I can't keep them straight.
Stepping back, it was around ten to twelve years old, my parents started putting me on a Trailways bus to visit my Grandparents two states away, in Arkansas. As it still is today, the interstate bus was basically the bottom wrung of transportation. Difference being, back then, the last eight rows of seats in the bus was the free-for-all section where the all seats had ash trays on the armrests and the bathroom was where you went to get high or grope a new friend.
I recently had the opportunity to ride the bus again and although the class structure placement of the clientele' hasn't changed, all else has. The look in the bus employee's eyes has gone from a lazy,
"I'm tired, so-what, Shut-up will ya?"
To a glassy eyed and stern "SHUT-UP or else!"

Definitely a more authoritarian feel. Armed security is the norm in the bigger bus stations nowadays and this can be felt in the attitudes of many bus employees.

In this book I share my most recent experience as I made a ring of the United States on foot with nothing but a backpack, a walking stick and a smile.
On this trip I hitch hiked, occasionally caught an interstate bus, and eventually got hooked on the new culture-shift phenomena of internet rideshare, I love it. All the while, even I am amazed at the people I've met and craziness encountered along the way.
It struck me to write about this particular trip, in this particular fashion, after reading a book I was recommended. During my first week of this very trip, my Uncle, on whose couch I was surfing, told me flat out, *"You have to read this Book!"*
"Uh, yeah, sure" was my standardized and somewhat mealy reply. But something in his eye said either he was going crazy, or the book had some sort of fatalistic attraction. After he mentioned it a few more times, I finally broke down and bought the "e" version for my traveling tablet. I finished it in spare time within the next week and through its typically convoluted twists of thought, started to see my travel in a different light. The book entitled **Car Sick** (*1) is an adventurous ramble on the exploits of the cult film Director, Author, John Waters as he experiments with hitch hiking and his vivid imagination. If you're a John Waters fan, his book won't disappoint. As far as I'm concerned, it's a recommended read. It took his book to help me gain an appreciation for what I have previously considered

everyday situations as being bizarre, scary and/or entertaining. Because some of the situations in this book are just that, and even more, half of the names have been changed to protect the "not so innocent." Unlike the John Waters book, **Car Sick** , *this* book is completely non-fiction.

So here's what John Waters inspired me to share...

A Curb Caste Experience

Chapter One

Ramp it Up

Not the usual place to start an adventure, I started out in the Arizona Desert. Most often in the desert are found tales of slow death, eggs cooked on concrete and an environment that would rather see you dead than sweat. Since most folks around here merely daydream of escaping this plight, I'd say no better place to start an adventure. A short explanation of how I got here might be in order to help lend a bit of perspective. I landed in this particular part of the desert as a result of a previous exodus, *"I gotta get the hell outa here,"* from a place in Arizona that was more of a high desert area and had a relatively milder climate. It wasn't the climate I left behind as uncomfortable. I'd been stuck in Tombstone, Arizona for a year and a half since my departure from the hospital in Las Vegas and I'd had enough of its charms to last a lifetime.

One of the bugaboos in America when traveling amongst the curb caste is that one has no choice but to interact with others who are also traveling and living cheaply.

It may be novel to find low cost means of travel, or it may be a necessity. Either way, if you ever consider jumping into this arena, you'll need to be diligent in your attention and as mentally prepared as a person can be. Many of the horrific incidents Americans watch on television news broadcasts these days quite often involve people living in this lower caste of society and this is the very group of people that cheap travel has us mingling with. Don't get me wrong, I don't want to paint our American society with broad strokes. But shall we just say, there is more of a dog-eat-dog, and paranoid attitude when money is scarce. In these crowds, mental illness is also more prevalent than in other groups of humans. Being aware of this before I began helped me to realize that I needed to blend-in as much as possible. I had to try and assimilate, even though I know there are also many in these crowds that prefer to prey on others of the same caste.

A while back I bought an older, smaller RV that had barely been used in its twenty-year life. Traveling in semi-comfort, I was supplementing my nest egg writing articles for various magazines. Buying low, selling high off Craigslist everywhere I stopped, generally enjoying visiting places and meeting new folks. That was fun. What wasn't fun was the occasional run-in with our societies negative elements, and one of these run-ins involved me being on the wrong end of a shotgun.

That isn't a tale for this book but more of a *tell* for you, the reader, as to where I've come from and the possibilities of the road. That incident landed me in the hospital in Las Vegas. After discharge, a friend I had met on the road during my previous year of travel offered me place to stay while I recovered. That place was Tombstone, Arizona.

To be "from" someplace, alludes that you are no longer there. In considering Tombstone, Arizona, when looking up from below, a more apt name for a plot of dirt there has never been. But looking back from beyond, it's a great place to be from.

After nearly two years, my savings torn away to pay for the hospital visit, I finally had a monthly stipend in the form of Social Security disability payments. It wasn't easy, but after a short while I learned how to live on such a small amount. It's actually not that difficult for me, I am even able to save a bit if I put my mind to it. Savings that eventually give way to my old friend, wanderlust.

Being of the minimalist mindset I looked around for a place where I could live within my means. I found a great natural community in a truly "Gilligan's Island" setting, the proverbial oasis in the desert. The only problem with my new roost, and everyone that lives there will agree, is that it is still *in* the desert. The Autumn, Winter and Spring are a coveted gift but Summer temperatures push one hundred and twenty degrees as a natural fact.

This slow roasting furnace starts up in late May and doesn't let up till the crack of October.
I landed at the oasis on the crack, October 1, 2015, and sunk right in to the paradisiac habits of the community. I was generally quite happy, until a few months later, I felt the itch. The itch had teamed up with troublesome stories of local summers to create a planning stage for my "Summer Vacation" away from this soon-to-be oven oasis. Not far from Tucson, not far from Phoenix, not far from Hades. Triangulate those three locations and you will find my starting point.
Open the door, Hansel, Gretel and I, are getting out.

The idea of a walking road trip started to take hold in April 2016 after a two and a half week National Parks hiking sojourn with a friend in Utah. It felt good to get back into the old routine of playing outdoors. Since it was starting to get toasty outside in Arizona, I dug out my travel gear, made a list, and had Amazon online deliver the items I still needed.
How much did I take? What did I take?
I used a high quality but not flashy 50-liter travel pack with internal stiffeners. I brought three changes of clothes *including* what I was wearing, and all the knick-knacks and necessities that would fit inside or strap on the outside. On a trip like this it's important to keep total carry weight in mind, I didn't want to be an inch or two shorter at the end of the trip. My pack was right at thirty-five pounds and I wouldn't recommend heavier than that for anyone on a long trip.

I spent good money on a quality pack, shoes, rain shell jacket, sleeping bag and mat. These are the items that need to be of the best quality. Sometimes friends, family and craigslist have hi-quality unused or lightly used pieces available cheap. I already had most of the items on my list and really only needed to buy a few things. When I left I still had $300 from my savings and my monthly stipend. Not much in the big picture but more than I actually needed. I expected to buy small things along the way but... thrift is my master.

Advice on preparedness if contemplating a similar trip would be to have water and to try and blend in, let the rest just happen. Nothing flashy, nothing bright and shiny-new to be seen, but top quality is needed. It's best to be clean-cut and not smelly.

When I think of myself at times deciding whether or not to pick up a hitch hiker, my own first consideration is the possibility of a foul smell or some type of grunge being rubbed into the passenger seat. A hitch hiker's look is very important. In a roundabout way, that is kind of how I look at the whole experience. Managing how people see me as to not attract attention in the crowd but to gain favor when needed. In todays judgmental society, I found that you'll be stuck on the corner of cornfield and fencepost to greet the cows-coming-home if you try to hitch a ride as a smelly, dirty mess. Likewise, entering a restaurant or any other public space a foot traveler uses becomes an issue if overly disheveled.

Another big consideration for many of us in our fear mongering society is the need for self-protection. It may seem absurd considering my past experiences but, No-Guns-For-Me.

No matter the past, I can only hope that if I bring no negativity with me, no negativity will find me. I carry only a couple generally useful knives that could be used for protection if necessary. No, not a sword, not a machete' or a bowie knife, and not even one that is kept on my belt. Any type of potential weapon openly displayed is perceived as an affront to those around us. It displays a person's level of paranoia and therefore their level of vulnerability.

Any knives I carry are put away, out of sight with one handy at all times but not seen. I also make a point not to routinely carry any drugs or alcohol. I figure the cops may talk to me a few times along the way, and going to jail for a random high isn't cool or necessary. That kind of stuff is always available and will find me along the way I'm sure.

By now, after so many years and dozens of times packing and eventually realizing I've forgotten something, I've learned to not worry about the small stuff. Letting things develop and happen on their own is often more satisfying in the end. I actually look forward, in some odd way to realizing that I forgot something at home or left something behind at a stop. I can't remember anyone ever saying they canceled their trip after only one day when realizing they forgot their

toothbrush… or even cell phone. These hiccups always work their way out, and how they do is often part of the fun.
Yes, this type of fun can be somewhat masochistic. You'll find in my travels, this becomes a theme. ☺

By mid May, my day of departure was planned and the route set in sand. I'd solicited sponsors for my road trip from friends on Facebook. My route was dotted with over twenty friends and family across the country that had reached out to offer a couch to surf, a ride through their town or even a dinner and catch-up session. It was decided my day of departure would be a Saturday. I'd get a one-way ride to our closest town on the community's Saturday supply run. This was the day on which every two weeks, the folks in my community go to the grocery store and take care of other general shopping business. The handful of people I live with in the desert oasis are a great bunch. Reactions when I told them my summer plans ranged from disbelief, to fear and envy, but all smiled and happily agreed that the heat can do terrible things to you in the summer months. I've often thought a few folks there at the oasis may be actual proof.
A week before leaving, I came to the realization that my laptop could not come along on this trip. Keeping it from harm would occupy my thoughts and the weight was too much. At the same time, my internet needs could not be met by the age of my eyes and the size of the screen on my smart phone. Easily remedied with a

little advanced warning but time was running short. I quickly ordered a cheap ten-inch tablet on Amazon whilst at the same time crossing my fingers and toes that it would arrive in time. There's no telling out here. Mail comes daily from all three major carriers but occasionally UPS packages are brought a day or two late by the U.S. Postman. It's a weird situation, kind of like the mailman mailing your mail to you.
So strange it must be true.

At four days till blast-off, I woke up fresh from a dream about a walking stick. This was a previous idea somehow forgotten. I'd spent a little time envisioning this and it must have been on a timer in my head. Somewhere on this land was waiting a nice piece of bamboo for a walking stick. I'd seen perfect examples I'd like, taken from one or another of the bamboo stands here. It took a while but eventually, after scouring all the stands on the property, I found the perfect piece. With the use of our fully equipped wood shop it was soon turned into a walking staff with great appeal. It turned out to be a pretty nice stick. So nice in fact, I spent a little time during my trip keeping this walking stick in my possession.

Everyone, including me, was bored on the Friday before my scheduled take off. My new tablet arrived the previous day and all my travel gear was packed and waiting. A look at the weather report showed it was going to be five degrees hotter the next day as the summer heat started to ascend so it was agreed the usual Saturday shopping trip would take place on Friday. This moved my departure up a bit, but what kind of schedule did I really have? I was already chomping at the bit and may have subliminally placed this idea in their heads anyway.

I was all about... "Let's Go!"

It was agreed I would go to town in the van with them. I would meander through the shopping chores then take part in the usual lunch ritual of Mexican food before being dropped off at the far end of town. Fine with me, a last bit of air conditioning and a good meal would be appreciated.

After getting everyone together and making sure this was going to happen, I headed back to the RV to retrieve my gear and close everything up. I must have gone over every bit at least three times. Everything was checked again, and I thought in earnest for a glimmer of anything I may have forgotten. I went through all the stuff in my head that creates worry when rushed and came out clean.

Within minutes we were packed up and gone from the oasis. A short time later, and not thirty seconds before pulling in to the Grocery store parking lot twenty-three miles from our front gate, I stifled a yell...

"OH SHit... I can't go"

It was almost too funny, and too real.

"I don't have my phone"

Five very embarrassing words.

After all the prep and to-do, after all the thought and ego put into this trip, to be humbled by these five measly words.

It may seem impossible or even ghastly to many people these days, but I, and most folks who live in my community, don't carry our cell phones on our person. There is only one service carrier that reaches all the way out to the oasis. Even then, to get a usable signal we must use a range extender kept in a shed on the property. This shed is called the phone shed. Many of us leave our phone inside so we can get messages and texts. This is where my phone was, on a shelf, blinking happily, in the phone shed.
"Better now than later," was my first thought. Then a little more panic by me, a few phone calls by clearer heads (dear Lynne actually brought her phone) and soon it was settled. Roughly forty-five minutes later, I was waiting in front of the bank when one of our neighbors, my phone in hand, rolled up. Luckily we caught our neighbor Bruce and his son Joe right before Joe was getting ready to leave for town. Joe graciously stopped by the oasis, picked up my phone from the phone shed and relayed it to me in town.
Joe's a pretty good guy.

See what I mean?... it works out.

With the phone debacle at rest, I felt a rush of confidence in my mission that carried me through the rest of the shopping and a nice leisurely farewell Mexi-lunch. Being every bit of 108 degrees outside and all the while mindful, at lunch I supplanted the hydration I would need for the next few hours with a trio of margaritas.

... Rocks, with salt please.

A Curb Caste Experience

Chapter Two

The Curb

As we rolled up to the far side of town where it was agreed my friends would leave me, brows furrowed and I found two of them looking at me for signs of apprehension.
They found none.
Nope, nada… zippo, I was ready.
With the water bladder in my pack full, mind fully lubricated by lunchtime imbibement alongside a twinge of the unknown, the van pulled away, and I waved goodbye.
As John Waters book would later reinforce, and I apparently intuitively knew, I had a few good signs made-up and ready to go.
"PHOENIX" and "NOT STINKY" were the first two signs I used and they worked like a charm. No more than ten minutes after being dropped off, I was looking around feeling the heat when a 1990's sedan, one rear window taped over with a plastic bag, pulled up. Front passenger window rolled down, the driver craned her neck leaning over the person sitting in the front seat and motioned for me to get in the back.

My First Ride! A big smile wouldn't go away. Inside I was yelling, "YAY_YEAH!!.... SKA_ORE.!!"
I could read my face in hers, she had a googly smile too. Linda seemed like a nice lady. She and her Native American boyfriend were on their way to Phoenix to visit family and said they would take me the entire way to Phoenix. She was a decent driver and kept her eye on me in the rearview while she talked about her life's inequities... front to back... non-stop. One of the troubles she droned on about that didn't sink in right away was how her daughter had stopped making payments on her car. The car Mom had signed for and given the down payment on. The car Mom had no keys to and had to repossess by breaking the rear window and ignition lock. The car now legally stolen, the car I was presently sitting in. When I saw the broken ignition lock, it sunk in.
The boyfriend didn't have much to say, in-fact he said nothing the entire way, not a peep. She did mention once that she hoped I didn't mind her lighting up a joint, "medicinally" of course. I was OK with that and hoped it would be passed back, "medicinally" of course, but she never did. Then about half way to Phoenix Linda looked over to her boyfriend, then up to the rearview at me.

> *"We're gonna stop to see someone along the way. I gotta drop you at the McDonalds on the corner, but if you're still there when we get back, we'll pick you up."*

What could I say? "Sounds good to me, Thanks."
It turned out to be a gas station, no McDuhs here.
Did I do or say something wrong?
Maybe my nods weren't quick enough, my eye contact too iffy in response to her rambles, maybe my face had given away my low interest level, hard to say. Coulda been that dude in the passenger seat was in need of another fix, or maybe another 40. He *was* after all completely and undeniably wasted on something.
Whatever it was made no matter.
Walking out to the road in front of the gas station, I plopped my pack and stick on the ground next to a shiny new penny, heads up.

"Find a penny on heads up,
and all day long you'll have good luck"

A little ditty that always comes back to me from my childhood, I couldn't help but pick it up. If the penny is tails up you're supposed to flip it over and leave the good luck for the next person but this one was on heads up so I reached down and picked it up. It was one of the new shield-back style. I'd never taken a real close look at these new pennies. Nowadays, when given pennies in my change, I usually pitch them in to the parking lot as I walk back to my car turning them into good luck pieces. While I was inspecting the shiny new slug, up pulls a new Ford truck.
I was stunned for a second.
"Wow," I couldn't remember that ditty ever working so well.

As I got in, my new chauffer Steve told me that he must have been destined to pick me up. He'd passed me back where I'd initially been dropped off outside Globe and felt bad for me because it was so hot. He'd turned around and back-tracked to pick me up but when he got back to the spot where I'd been standing, I was gone.

> *"Crazy huh? I stop for gas and here you are again. Must be fate."*

"Yeah, that is strange," is all I could muster thinking back to the penny. Steve was in his late twenties, straight laced and working a good job at a local copper mine. I was the first hitch hiker he'd ever picked up. By the time we rolled into the Mesa/Phoenix area he felt sorry to drop me off in the heat and ignored my urging to do so. He graciously insisted on taking me to the light rail station. There I could get on the air-conditioned cross-town train which would take me as far West in the Phoenix area as I needed.

He dropped me off across from a light rail platform but not before getting my picture. I understood of course, I took his as well. I resolved to get a pic of everyone that gave me a ride and I can only imagine picking up your first hitch hiker is also a photo worthy event, especially since I let him keep his head and all.

Standing on the street corner I looked around for a minute, apparently there was something going on nearby that required costume. The sidewalks were a curious sight, smattered with teens through thirty-somethings, dressed in what I could only imagine were characters from some level of comic or cartoon worship.

Lifting my pack over one arm I walked up the stairs to one of the many platforms that seemed to extend into the horizon along Main Street. I was trying to decipher the instructions at the light rail ticket kiosk and had just decided it was time to find my glasses when a middle aged guy with a kept yet scraggly appearance sidled up next to me with his arm extended,

"Here man, I got this."

and handed me a daily free pass for the light rail. Before I could ask him any questions or thank him he skipped away with a wave.

"No sweat man, I'm lucky, you're lucky, we're all lucky."

I stood there in a quandary, amazed that he just quoted me a line from my all-time favorite cult movie (*2). Stunned, I waved back and lightly yelled "Thanks man!... the banisters lucky!" but not really loud enough for him to hear as he moved away.

Looking at the ticket slip in my hand, then back up at him moving down the platform, I pondered the recent events. Sitting down in the heat to wait on the next train I was in a state of mind fuzz, strange and ooky events were piling up. I was studying the schedule map to see how far I could go through the Phoenix area when the train pulled up and the *trip* continued. The train car doors slid open, and like another scene from

Rocky Horror, inside was packed full of elaborately costumed characters. Squeezing in and around the garish costume plumage and finding a seat open for no apparent reason, I sat down. I could almost picture myself as a cartoon traveler amongst them, one with a funny hat and a long feather, maybe wearing lederhosen. I still had the shiny shield-back penny in my front left pocket. I fondled it through the canvas of my hiking shorts almost expecting Rod Serling to show up next to narrate the rest of my day (*3).

By studying the map schedule I could see that after several stops and about thirty minutes the train would take a jog north then turn around for the eastbound trip. Not needing to go further north, I got off at an appropriate stop, donned my pack for the first time, and started walking. The streets were full of cars and there were people mulling around everywhere. Plenty of folks looked at me walking down the sidewalk in the middle of Phoenix with my pack as if I were lost, and I sorta was. I didn't really have a clear view in my head of where I was or where I was going. It was mid-afternoon and hot as hell so I walked up to a Starbucks and went in to plan my next move on my tablet and get a stiff ice coffee.

As I would do a hundred more times, I utilized Google Maps. Cooling down and studying the screen, I figured to walk as far west as I could go and still be at a good highway on-ramp before finding a spot to sleep. After a few minutes of air-conditioned rest, I got back on the street and walked, and then walked some more. That day I probably put in ten miles and as the sun continued to fall I started looking for a place to sleep. I'd previously decided to stay in a motel only once a month as a luxury if I felt so inclined so I needed to get a grip on finding a place to hide away safely for the evening. Along the way I passed a high school and noticed it was completely surrounded by a tall metal fence. Not the chain link style, but heavy iron bar with points on the tips. It seemed that all the buildings and houses within eyesight were either walled up or had bars on the windows and doors. This did not give me a warm fuzzy feeling about my security as darkness approached. Walking past the school I saw the parking lot gate was open and since dusk was upon me, I walked right in like I belonged there. Looking around, there were no signs of people anywhere so I figured this would be a great place to lay low for the evening. After a look around the sprawling property I headed towards the football field and decided under the bleachers was a safe bet. I took off my pack, found a good spot and settled in. As I was looking around, eating a bit of food from my pack and sipping from my water bladder, my eyes kept returning to the press box above me. On a whim I crept up the bleachers trying to stay out of the security lights that had come on around me and found the press box unlocked. What luck! Before long my gear was moved and I settled in. After locking the door from the inside, it felt very secure.

My first day behind me, I was quite proud of myself. That lucky penny had done its job for sure.

In the morning around 5am I woke, gathered my things and skulked towards the gate I'd come in through the previous night only to find that it had been closed and locked sometime after I'd arrived. Dread passed over me as I stared at the all-encompassing twelve foot, spear topped iron fence. I was locked in.
What to do? Call someone? Yell? It seemed obvious that when found inside a locked schoolyard as a vagrant I'd find myself in the slam for the rest of the weekend at the very least. Not a good start to my journey for sure. That damned penny!

There's a very pithy and wise saying in here somewhere... beware the penny ditty.

It was just before dawn and still dark, so I did the only thing a trapped rat could do. I scurried around the perimeter staying in the shadows as not to be seen from the surrounding streets and apartments. Luckily the fence changed to chain link behind an area in the back of the sports fields. Here it joined at an angle where a gate was firmly locked but was just janky enough to ascend and get over... for the average person. Unfortunately I am no longer an average person. I may have mentioned that I'm now on disability. The reason for this is that my right arm doesn't work well anymore and I have a bit of vertigo. After sweating the load for a few minutes and visualizing myself in the hospital with my good arm handcuffed to a bed rail, I sucked it up. Changing my visualization to cresting the fence, and with herculean effort, made it to the top, mostly with eyes closed. Pant leg caught on top, I nearly fell as I went over but pulled free, then jumped to the ground with the added pack weight nearly breaking my back. After retrieving my walking stick from under the fence I quick-step-hopped down the walkway and got back on my way. West young man... West.

During this trip I found that my best bets were stopping at Denny's, McDonalds and Starbucks, likenesses being rest, air conditioning and Wi-Fi. You can always count on a clown burger every several miles and that morning after a few paces underfoot I spotted the arches. Seeing the big red and yellow sign also serves as a mini-goal since the arches towering above can generally be seen a mile or two off in the distance. After stopping for coffee, muffin and bathroom use, I put my nose down and continued. There were, "West to LA" and "Not Stinky" signs stuck into my pack on the back and my thumb was out while walking the entire time but, no-luck. All said, I put in several more miles that day in horrendous heat, stopping only twice. Once for a water refill and once to rest and share a couple beers in front of a convenience store with a stranded cholo (*4) having woman problems. His girl had abandoned him there after finding he had not only cheated on her but was holding out on the second half of his weekly paycheck. Poor guy, all he had left was half a paycheck and a lowrider full of his compadres coming to pick him up. Gauging his smile when they showed up, I'd say that was all he needed for now.

By that time it was around 4 in the PM and the heat was brutal, so considering my state of tired I started looking around for my evening resting spot. While on the look, I passed another Mickey Dees and used their Wi-Fi to do what anybody in my shoes would do. I planned my way out. I got on my tablet and typed in the words I'd hoped wouldn't find me this soon... "G-r-e-y-h-o-u-n-d." I wanted to get to LA, but more specifically, to the coast asap to get out of the heat. Daydreams of surf and breeze kept me going this whole day and I'd talked myself into thinking that the end would justify the means. I also hadn't been on the interstate bus for many years and was curious to see if the seats were still sticky.

The nearest Greyhound pickup was in a small town outside Phoenix named Tolleson. With the miracle of modern communication I called and talked to father time about schedules. I mean this guy sounded very old, I could actually hear this dude decomposing over the phone. It was a very slow, unnerving conversation but when finally over I figured I was good for the 1pm to Los Angeles the next afternoon. It would be great to stand in front of him at his Insurance Office / Bus Station the next day to see how well my imagination of this guy matched up with reality. I like ancient folks, I like to try to read their life from their faces. Sometimes they make me feel good about my own state of decomposition... sometimes.

If I was going to get there in time I'd have to put a mile or two in tonight and another five or so in the morning. I got on it, and after a couple miles walking found a place along the road with a wooded area that was next to a big gas station convenience store, next to a Home Depot, next to a... YES, another school!

This one was a smaller private school, more like a grade school Montessori, set back off the road with a short fence to match. As I walked down the side street around back I found a large group of people there apparently from the neighboring apartment complex. They were sitting on the benches staring at their phones taking advantage of the schools open Wi-Fi network. This made the school unsuitable for my purposes but the adjacent wooded area behind the Home Depot looked promising. Once there, I found the Home Depot didn't have a fence along back around their storage area and the automatic lights surrounding the building that had just started to come on, weren't working in the corner making for a nice little resting spot between pallets. The sun was going down and I was sure I hadn't been spotted getting back there so I felt secure enough to leave my pack and stick hidden under some debris. I was going to the convenience store for a beer before it got too dark.

The lot beside the store was a hangout for a large group of Latinos drinking and enjoying loud Mexican folk music. As I passed, several noticed me and we exchanged the requisite nods. On my way back I popped one of the two beers I'd purchased and stood there for a minute checking out their fun, once again exchanging nods before moving on. Setting up my sleeping gear among the clutter behind Home Depot was quick and easy. I moved a few pallets and boxes around to make a covered hideaway.

The sun was nearly gone and it was around eight thirty when all of a sudden there was the sound of voices coming from inside the Home Depot building. They were coming from behind a huge roll-up door just a few feet away and talking with an intensity that made my hair stand on end. I was hidden from view, but when the huge door began to roll-up, I started looking for exits. It was all happening too fast so I froze right there as two employees came outside to smoke and talk. They were conversing, walking around the area stacking bags of dirt and moving pallets around with a hand jack. One of them came over to within two feet of my hiding cubby and grabbed one of the pallets covering my spot. The effort and forward motion kept her from glancing behind after picking up the pallet but if she had, or if the other worker had been close, I was right there, easily seen underneath. Luckily they were apparently finishing up for the evening as the store was now closing.

Their attention was elsewhere and I was able to remain right there in the same spot with a good nights sleep. It was kind of like going to bed after a scary movie. I replaced the pallet after their departure and in the morning left it there on purpose wondering if either would notice the pallet they moved had mysteriously returned itself.

By the way... Paula, I don't think she's leaving you. That's jealousy talking, you'll work through it, you know how you girls are. ☺

The next morning there was a mile or two of walking till I found a Denny's for a light breakfast. After breakfast and cleanup I started out again on a long walk through an industrial area and was finally able to take a rest before the realization of my next hiccup.
It was around 10:30am on a Sunday morning. A fact that had failed to enter my mind, until I stood on the sidewalk in front of an Insurance Office/Greyhound Bus stop, closed-up tight.
The old guy had gone through the entire routine with me. He told me I couldn't purchase a ticket over the phone, it had to be in person or on the website. I'd hung up with him and got on my tablet to try and purchase the ticket online but my zip code was giving their system fits so I resigned to buying the ticket in person without thought to the fact that the next day would be Sunday.
I went to the convenience store next door to refill my water bladder then came back and sat down in front of

the insurance building. A bus pulled up a few minutes later. The driver assumed I was sitting there waiting for his arrival but it turned out that bus was heading to San Diego. The driver was a real nice guy and told me that if I wanted, he would let me on and I could pay for the ticket at the next open stop. He was worried about leaving me in the heat till the next days buses pulled through. After a very short thought, the priority of my destination was replaced by heat and frustration.
I thought for about two seconds... *"San Diego isn't that far from Los Angeles."* It was an easier decision than most challenging predicaments usually present. I took him up on his offer and got on the bus.

Uncle Chris, my Moms brother, lives in beautiful San Diego. I hadn't planned on going there since I was there recently for a visit in February, but the fickle finger of fate lightly pushed me in that direction so I decided to enlist my mantra of freedom and "just let things happen."
The buses today are the same, but so much different. The rest room in back is now merely an open hole to a sloshing blue disturbance with no water or other amenities available. There is more room to move around in the cabin and the seats are nicer than I remember. There are electric plugs at every row of seats to run and charge todays electronics and mother of all surprises... there is Wi-Fi on every bus! Later, as I traveled again on the Greyhound I came to the realization that Wi-Fi on the buses is more to sooth the

savage breast of their riders and was probably worth its weight in jigabits in the prevention of many forms of debauchery that would be present without it. While traveling down the road, the cabin of the bus was completely quiet sans the standard buzzes, dings and beeping of modern electronics. As I found to be par throughout my entire journey, including the bus, nearly everyone had their face buried in a phone, tablet or laptop.

Screen addiction was rampant and after awhile it becomes off-putting. It just seems un-natural... and kind of rude.
While on the bus I joined the masses and called Uncle Chris in San Diego. I was lucky he was even there considering his busy schedule. All was good and with no more than a four-hour heads up, he welcomed me at the Greyhound depot.

A Curb Caste Experience

Chapter Three

West Coast Breeze

Wow! What a change !!

I boarded the Bus outside Phoenix at a sweltering 114 degrees and got off the Bus in San Diego at a perfect 68. Beautifully mild and pepper tree heavenly, San Diego has a wonderful climate. It felt so good I took a purposefully dramatic breath and big sigh after retrieving my pack from the luggage storage under the bus. For some reason, perhaps my heat fixation had something to do with it, I believe San Diego is the end-all for having the perfect climate. I've been there a few times now and the weather has been fantastic. Although a world-class anthill in its own right, San Diego's burb areas seemed light on traffic and leisurely. At least that's my completely heat stroked observation.

I spent a few days with my Uncle, Aunt and Cousin. We had a great time reminiscing, pondering the future and enjoying the imbibement that comes with family and like minds. We're a strange podge, my Uncle being only four years older than myself, my Aunt not far

from the same and my Cousin being less than half my age. Although extremely different in many ways... we connect. That's why I eventually read John Waters book Car Sick after Chris mentioned it. He was right, the book was strange, pertinent and changed my perspective on what I was personally doing at that moment in my life...
Yeah !! I love it when that happens!

It was a beautiful weekday morning when I left San Diego. Eventually duty called and Uncle took an Uber to the airport heading out on a business trip. The entire time while there I had been dabbling in Craigslist rideshare but hadn't figured out the nuances yet. My first try at a ride turned out to be a no-show. There seemed to be a lot of profiteers on there also. After researching Google maps I realized it would be a hassle to thumb my way out, so I took the bus to Los Angeles. I had a timeline to meet for getting to Santa Barbara to see an old friend and I wanted to leave good time to spend in the middle. I had two other potential sponsors just north of L.A. with timelines that unfortunately didn't work out, but all things work out in the end right? If things don't work out, you know it's not the end.
Isn't that how it goes?
I'd never been to more than the Los Angeles airport on layovers but I felt like I'd been there before. Not surprising I guess, considering half the shows on TV are filmed there.

Los Angeles proved to be exactly what I'd imagined as I walked from the Greyhound depot. I easily found a Craigslist rideshare placed that morning by a San Diego surfer dude looking to get to Big Sur on the cheap by sharing rides. I was also planning on going to Big Sur, just not right now. Later, I would think back on this ride perhaps wishing I'd taken it all the way to Big Sur but right now, being dropped off at a Santa Barbara exit was exactly what I was looking for. I had to walk a mile or so to get to the pick-up point but had plenty of time. For some reason, as I walked around taking in my surroundings, I imagined myself walking around in Randy Newman's "I love L.A." music video. That song stayed in my head for three days, helping to define musical torture. A curse from early MTV.

"Bro," as I'll call him, wasn't exactly a brilliant conversationalist but he drove with the best. I ended up in Santa Barbara two days early. My friend wasn't back from her own leisure trip and had only two days at home before having to leave again so at least I wasn't late. Being two days early I can surely be at our meet-up on time, right? She lived in the UCSB north end of Santa Barbara, in a town named Goletta near the airport. It turned out that my understanding of her saying "just north of town," actually meant several miles. A mile is a very different thing under foot than in a car, especially when you string fourteen of them together.

I was happy to exit surfer dudes car but misjudged

the location of my exit on the highway by not mapping the address before hand. The better side of my error was that downtown Santa Barbara is very nice. As I walked through the downtown area, the entire district appeared to be an outdoor mall of high-end shops and night clubs.

It was dusk, about 8pm, and in the midst of this luxury I was starting to notice a lot of homeless folks up and down the streets. Just as dark was setting in, I walked up to an open corner bench area and was accosted by a group of three vagabond dudes. Jimmy, the scraggliest of the three was proudly displaying a huge magnum Champagne bottle his buddy Leon had shoplifted at a nearby drug store. I must admit I found it impressive that someone could shoplift a bottle so big. Terry, a bearded and completely wacked out traveler, sat talking to an unnamed imaginary friend and had a guitar sitting on the bench next to him. After disappointing them on their hopes of a cigarette, I sat down and joined in their despair. We shared the huge champagne bottle, held a dirt weed joint closely, and talked shit about everyone that passed. The cops passed bye a few times but we saw them coming and just gave them a Sears catalog pose (spring collection) and they drove on.

Terry had always wanted to learn to play the guitar so when he got a windfall he bought one at a pawnshop, it wasn't a bad one either, an 80's model Yamaha.

There was no case to protect it and it wasn't in tune but he reminded me,

> *"Even Bruce Springsteen started somewhere maaan. It'd be cool if I could sit out here on the bench and play songs to folks as they walk bye and Jeffrey can dance, It'd be cool."*

I guessed Jeffrey was his imaginary friend.
Terry's reasoning was hopeful and sound, and I really loved the mental picture it conjured up.
I tuned it up for him after downloading a tuner App on my phone and showed him how to play an easy three-chord song, The Romantics, *"What I like about you."* We all took a turn around the corner behind the bushes with a little wax I'd brought with me from San Diego then sung that song raucously for thirty minutes changing the words to what we liked about everything,
"We like your shoes..."
<u>Buskin' for Nuthin'</u> was the name of our impromptu super group. All sorts of people in cars and on foot stared on blankly, trying to ignore us, imagining we weren't there. That would have made a great video. It was as if we were ghosts trying our best to reach through the veil to rattle our chains, but to no avail, nobody even accidentally looked our way till well past. After hearing of my travels and future plans, Leon told me all about his adventures riding the rails across the country on freight trains. He made it sound so good this book nearly included a train chapter. He explained that there are places where long train strings stop and

wait for oncoming traffic to pass before their turn comes to use the rails. Leon tells me you jump in a freight car while its stationary, and at worst, have to jump out at 5mph as it stops somewhere you either want to get off or must get off. Sometimes you must get off due to railroad security empty car inspections at points along the way looking for parasitic travelers. Several hundred miles per trip for free sounds pretty good across desolate swaths of terra like Montana, Wyoming and Nebraska.
Foot and car traffic started to wane around ten-ish and the cops became more present so I took some sage advice from my new compadres and headed toward the Catholic Church. They informed me that here in Santa Barbara the cops couldn't harass a homeless person on church grounds unless called by the church. I don't consider myself homeless but I spent the night at the church behind some ornamental bushes with no disturbance and was fine.

The University of California Santa Barbara (UCSB) is what the north end is all about. There is a lot going on, and even more homeless folks hanging around. I had plans to meet my friend the next day so had a bit of time to kill. Finally able to realize the dream, I started walking towards the ocean to get in some beach time. Along my northbound walk I could occasionally see the water and I was ensconced in the waft of salty sea air. I flashed back several times to my Navy days with the smell of salt air all around.

It's amazing how scents from long ago can take you away within seconds.
I soon found myself walking down the street through neighborhoods and dorm areas. College kids were messing around here and there and I noticed a few homeless types hanging around. Passing an older lady walking her dog I put on a nice smile and gave her a greeting. As I spoke, she looked toward me and cringed then turned away with a horrific look of fear. This startled me because I had been trying to be neat and presentable the whole time, and I'm sure I was. I didn't smell or look messed up in any way. Later during my visit I was informed that Santa Barbara and Goletta had experienced an influx of homeless people wandering around during the last few years and many folks in town were frightened and disgusted with them. The town had enacted several measures to try and keep them away but instead, all efforts seemed to keep them trapped there. Santa Barbara's big money apparently hasn't gone hand in hand with big compassion. I discovered later in my travels that there are great examples from municipalities all over the country for them to follow.
We have a large homeless issue in the US and most likely always will. We should be able to get smart, be kind, and deal with it more effectively. It's a fact, you can't rid yourself of your perceived negatives by adding more negativity.

After shaking off my shake-off I eventually found a great spot in the reeds on a dune above the beach. It was serene and secluded with no people to be seen for a quarter mile around. There was a little trash waiting for me to pick up but there would be no worries from my presence. No campfire, No damage, I always take what I bring and leave no trace.

A few quick texts set me up to meet my friend the next morning at eight so I sat back into my spot, read a few chapters (I brought four hardcopy books with me), enjoyed a little after hours mind fog and fell deep asleep. It must've been the salt air because the morning sun didn't even wake me. When I finally did wake, the clock on my phone startled me sober displaying 7:40am. I had an immediate rush of adrenalin that sprung me into action. Ten minutes to pack up, another fifteen to get back on the streets and another forty five minutes to get to our meeting spot makes Mike a late boy.

Aaah! I really dislike being late. It was driven into my brain in the military and ever since has been a pet peeve. Luckily a lot of folks don't feel the same way (never thought I'd say that) and within a few minutes I was able to straighten it all out by phone. She was running late as well and obliged by coming to pick me up while I was walking back into town. I spent the next two days lounging poolside at April's condo complex, eating well and enjoying much. Then came the morning of the third day when I was dropped off at the Goletta

Micky Dees and reality changed back to skulking the California roads.
Going inside I ordered what turned out to be my road standard breakfast, coffee and a muffin, took my pack to a table, sat down and started perusing rideshare listings. Within five minutes the manager was in front of me telling me I needed to take my pack outside. I was seated at a table with four chairs and my pack on the table must have set off the Santa Barbara / Goletta homeless alarm. Not wanting to help reinforce his already boorish stereotype, I moved quietly to a two-chair table and put my pack on the floor. This wasn't good enough for him, but since I had no aire of guilt, I'd paid for food, and the restaurant wasn't even half full, I was happy he opted for discretion. Still, it was a bit of a display. I felt like yelling, "*Yeah folks ! All Eyes on ME Please !!*" but of course they already were.
Its strange to me that "homeless reefer madness" takes such a deep hold that many folks, money or not, can't recognize the difference between a homeless person and a traveler. I'm now pretty sure that a "traveler" to most people in the U.S. has come to mean that this person doesn't have enough money for a car or even a bus ticket, so this must equate to a homeless derelict on foot. After all, "Why would anyone walk?"
Unfortunately my observation of these condescending people is also an uncomfortable and stereotypical judgment. I'm more than happy to set the example for a responsible traveler on foot, but even my hardened

attitude about an in-check ego was being attacked here. I imagined, apparently incorrectly, that most Americans can tell the difference between a thousand dollars worth of outdoor gear strapped to a jaunty outdoor type and an old book bag full of used Kleenex dragged around by a fly magnet, But No.

Yeah, that's harsh, and I don't really mean it, but here between these lines is where I get to vent.

Anyway... hitching didn't work well there.

I spent all day at a spot two blocks away from the highway which was not good at all for getting a ride. I wagged "ITS OK I'M WITH THE BAND" and "NOT HOMELESS, TRAVELLING NORTH," to no avail. I changed them around every so often but the originality and ingenuity of my signs, although prodding smiles from passing motorists, did me no good. The highway areas had been re-arranged so it was illegal to be on foot anywhere near them. A local told me this was another anti-homeless tactic gone awry. It certainly doesn't help. How are the people without wheels that you don't want there supposed to leave? Humph.

That evening I passed by the same McDingles on my way to the grocery store to get my evening meal. At the corner out front was a well-worn lady panhandling from the stopped cars at the traffic light. At the outdoor table in front of the McNarly's entrance door was a matching guy bumming from patrons as they emerged. They appeared to be a team, somehow I could tell they were together.

Thought to self : *"Good deed time"*

I went up and sat down at the table next to the dude at the door. After trying me out and finding I was a no-go, he chatted me up about he and his "wife" out on the corner. According to him, they'd been in the area twelve years and had hit hard times. They were Catholic and only ate fish on Fridays so they were bumming a little money to get a proper McFish meal for each of them. Nothing he said was congruent starting with the fact that the day was not actually Friday. The conversation was hard to follow and a bit painful. I was beginning to feel empathy for the manager inside when I blurted out,

> "I'm going over to the grocery store across the lot over there. Why don't you go with me and I'll set you up with a bunch of food? I've got a SNAP card with plenty on it and you guys can take a rest for awhile."

His answer blew me away,

> *"Naw that's ok, were only eating fish today.*
> *I'll take a couple bucks instead though."*

No man, I'm talking about $20 or $30 dollars worth of food here. You can buy some fish if you want.

> *"Thanks but I don't think she'd like that.*
> *I'll take the money though."*

What else could I do? Exasperated, I stood up with a confused look and walked to the grocery leaving the conditional pescetarians behind.

Yes, empathy and compassion, empathy and compassion... for all, including the town.

That night, although tempted, I did not have fish, I enjoyed an avocado, trail mix and a container of coconut water during a stirring sunset overlooking the Santa Barbara airport. My perch provided a perfect view of sunset and airport lights blending as in a kaleidoscope; all-in-all a pretty good night. I had found a ride on Craigslist the previous day and the next morning was back at Clown Burger waiting for the ride to come through... it never did. No call, no text, nothing to let me know of any changed plans. Whoever it was wouldn't even respond to my texts. After the realization of being stood-up hit me, I tried again, but this time went to the nearby Starbucks to sit and suck up free Wi-Fi... and not-so-free coffee.

It didn't take very long before I found a new listing by a university student going home to San Francisco on break. When she heard where I was, she offered to pick me up at the McRestaurant in an hour. With nothing better to do, I was early and stood on the side of the building waiting for her to show.

When she was a few minutes late I started to think... *she'll be looking for a guy with a pack*. My homeless friend was again fishing up front and had a small backpack. Maybe she pulled through, saw him, thought he was me and rolled on! That dude looked a little rough, I wouldn't blame her if that were the case... but thankfully it wasn't.

She texted that she was running a little late so I went up front and stood not too far from him until she arrived a short time later. So after only an hour or so and another slight scare of rejection, a very tall 20 something pulled up in a Subaru wagon and my journey continued.

Lauren (at one time my favorite female name) is studying at the University with the intention of working for the U.S. Forest Service. Such a tall, thin, well-built girl might look for a scholarship at UCSB in their Beach Volleyball program. Although she would have been a good scout for the team, this was not discussed. I recounted a story about an ex-family member that was once in the Forest Service. We talked about music, her aspirations, San Francisco and much more. It was a long trip. I wanted to know why she used Craigslist rideshare offering rides to strangers. At that time her answers were what I would have thought typical, but after many trips have found, are just great reasons. Cutting her carbon footprint in half, saving money by splitting how much money we spend on corporate oil.

She has a vetting process for riders responding off Craigslist (apparently I passed) that starts with the level and writing style of the responder. She's never had a real bad experience but recounted a couple unsavory ride adventures that I might have counted as bad. She also dislikes sleepers, having alert company was another big reason for finding passengers.

Her car got good mileage so we stopped for gas only once. I put in $20, which was nearly a tank full, much more than just half the gas she was asking for the trip. I asked if she would be interested in driving to Big Sur but after looking at the map and considering future plans and timing, I decided to skip Big Sur and for an easy point of reference had her drop me off at the San Francisco Greyhound terminal since it was downtown and not far from the water. They also have free Wi-Fi in the Greyhound terminals. It turned out this particular terminal was patrolled and highly regimented by underpaid yet very vocal security guards. Without a ticket on one side of the chain, or the forward motion of somehow obtaining a ticket on the other side, *"you gotta move along."*

There was a female security guard with a disturbingly precise helmet weave that took no prisoners. I opened my tablet with the Greyhound website in one window and hurriedly looked at CL rideshare listings going to my next destination in another. That night in San Francisco I opted to stay at a Hostile, it just seemed like the thing to do. San Francisco always works me up into a Haight/Ashbury romanticism for the angst of the past. Besides, some hostiles there have a unique look and although not free, or even very low cost, are the cheapest rooms or "beds in a dorm" that you'll find in the city. I needed a shower and a safe place to store my gear while I explored a bit.

San Fran was ok I guess, I've been there several times.

Nothing stood out or happened that was unusual for San Francisco. In my experience, typical of a destination city. It's us visitors that usually stir things up a bit, giving our destination a reputation, and I didn't feel like instigating just then.

That night I went to a bar whose menu included all the menu's from the local take-out joints, laminated and strung together on a brass ring. After a few drinks and some pretty bad Thai food from god-knows-where, I got back to the flop house safely and slept well.

My next days start was a little after five. There were fourteen blocks to walk to get to my pick-up point and four hours to get there, a cakewalk. I stopped in at a Starbucks for a latte' and scone, set up my tablet and found I'd been jilted again. This rideshare stuff is nearly as hit-and-miss as hitch hiking but at least this guy contacted me with a reason. Luckily there were several more listings heading to Sacramento so it didn't take long to set the wheels rolling again. I was starting to like this internet and text communication stuff, but not necessarily the emotional rollercoaster it rides in.

About two hours later Devon was right on time at 11am. He picked me up on a park bench overlooking the bay a short walk away. The sensory overload from that view was intense. The bridge, the fog, water and city... I almost wished him not to show. Curbside master-view pick-up service and he turned out to be the perfect ride to the door step of my next sponsor.

Devon said that he would go to his parents home just outside the eastern edges of Sacramento every weekend as long as he could get someone else to pay for the gas. I was happy to pay, in his Honda it was about eight bucks. He didn't have a lot of gas money but he did have a lot of weed. We were blitzed rolling till he dropped me in front of my friend's house on the outskirts of Sacramento later that afternoon.

Like I said, a perfect ride. Definitely worth the sawbuck I gave him for gas.

Bill and Darlene are a couple I'd met several years back on the North Fork of the Feather River in California. I was there at an area called Caribou for a couple months while writing a story for a Gold Prospecting publication. The local miners were giving me the low down on sniping gold nuggets from bedrock cracks and Bill and Darlene were staying near me at the same RV park. They were on vacation spending their days fishing and panning the river. Back then we barbequed every night and grabbed every beer from Bill's huge bottomless cooler. This night we did the same thing with the outrageously large cooler still in service, now on the rear deck of their woodsy Sacramento home. Bill followed me on Facebook and responded to my travel news with an offer of a nights stay and a good meal. As promised, we ate and drank well, caught up on each others lives and slept like a pile of logs. In the morning around seven, Bill and I had breakfast and then he dropped me at a promising

corner in Sacramento on his way to work.
I love those two, I truly hope to see them again. They were great, but Sacramento itself was a bit painful. It's here I started earning my current curb cred. I imagined it was payback for having such a charmed trip up until now. I imagined it would all come to an end with the next passing car. It didn't matter what I imagined, I was wrong. As it turns out, Sacramento is A-typical of the city attitude I'd moved to the nethers to avoid. Aaand... here I was hitching in the middle of it. Here is where I started taking a tally. Here is where I was given the opportunity to reaffirm my own closely held social stereotypes.
Since I have completed this trip as I write this, and because it was nearly an identical situation everywhere I went throughout the country, I can confidently pronounce to you with personal certainty... as a species, We-Are-Doomed.
How can one of my brilliantly crafted cardboard signs be effective if people rarely look up from their phones? There were at least two hundred cars passing me every thirty minutes. I stood just down the curb in a dedicated highway on-ramp entrance lane to I-5 north. At least eighty percent of the drivers that passed were either actively on their cell phone talking or had it in one hand staring at it while only occasionally glancing at the road. I was kind of disappointed because I had made a brilliant sign that I just knew would create lines of cars vying to pick me up.

Not only was my sign humorously intriguing, it was also interactive.
"WORLDS MOST INTERESTING MAN" wagging at cars got a few smiles from those that weren't buried in their phones but no-one even gave me the chance to speak the tag line...
"I don't always hitch a ride, but when I do, it's with you." (*5)
I thought that to be so clever, like a stepping stone to the art of hitching. Uma Thurman and her big thumbs would have been proud... oh well. (*6)
After a few hours, thoroughly dejected, I walked a few miles to another on-ramp area where I encountered new forms of local abuse. One car in particular made a game of me. Circling the block, a car full of High School kids passed me four times, each time visiting a different pestilence upon me.
The first round, it was un-intelligible jeers... *yeah, ok.*
The second time round' I got a goose on the throttle as they approached and a round of put-downs as they passed bye, *"Get A Car!!"* was the most original.
"Yeah, sure, Screw Off ... buncha punks," I murmured to myself as they turned the corner. The third time past was about fifteen minutes later with more jeers and small change thrown from the windows, this time involved all of them at once including a waft of skunkiness blowing past me to which I could only look after them and shrug with arms outstretched,
"What the fuck?"

I thought I recognized this game. Its one I'd played as a youth. You don't know what to-do but in lieu of anything else... more of the same. I didn't expect the fourth round, but when I saw their car approaching a few minutes later, I struggled with how to play with them. Escalating sucked, I didn't want push to come to shove. I fake jumped in front of their car, the driver laid on the horn. I pulled back and gave them the raspberries as they slowly passed, the front female passenger gave me a tit check, again yelling *"Get a Car!"* and someone else inside screamed something about a cop. At that point a couple things were thrown out the rear window at me, one lightly bouncing off my shoulder. If I could effectively throw a rock with my left arm I would've picked one up right then and hurled it. Knowing that I couldn't, I still bent down to find a rock and at least mime the part. When I looked down, there it was at my feet. One of the things tossed out the window at me was a small Wendy's soda cup with the top purposefully crunched and folded over. There was a garbage can chained to a bus stop sign there at the corner so I went to toss it in and felt a lite rattle from inside. Gingerly unfolding the top with one eye closed and head cocked back... there inside was a nice size and very crusty bud. My attitude changed in a millisecond. I looked after their car to give a wave but it was gone.

Aaah, not "Cop"... Cup.

What a nice bunch of little fuckers.

But there was more than one thing thrown out the window. Maybe another present was waiting. I looked around on the ground and curb from every angle but found nothing else except more pennies and trash. Frustration peaked and relieved, it was a sign, a sign that my day should be over. I headed in the direction of what looked like the last viable on-ramp. Not long after, I came across a commercial building with a large caged generator outside. I had scouted a few of these as potential sleeping areas but so far each had been locked, this one wasn't. It turned out to be a great spot and I slept well except for the fact that it was right next to the building's side entrance door. The door used by the employees coming to work at four in the morning. A lot of employees, seemingly all at once. Several of them had time to lean against the generator cage smoking before going in. They stood barely two feet from me, separated only by chain link with a vision strip weave, I huddled there in fearful déjà vu from my Home Depot incident. The stream of people showing up, going in, and standing there smoking lasted about an hour. As the string of employees subsided I was finally able to get out to the road without being seen and just as I was putting on my pack, an older Toyota truck with a beat-up looking topper stopped short as it passed me. The driver jumped out quickly, giving me a start but I was soon smiling as big as she was, we were wearing the same shirt. My green tie dye, Grateful Dead hitching shirt from the Oregon Country fair had caught Diane's eye from a block away. She saw my pack and sign, and even though she was only going another mile or two to pick up produce for the local food bank, she offered me a ride to the next on-ramp area. Diane was happy as a clam to see the shirt and someone wearing it of a like mind. When we arrived at the next on-ramp area we just sat there for a few minutes in a gas station parking lot talking about Oregon and our pasts, it was almost like we were old friends. I wonder if solidarity in under garments can be counted as a means of attraction for hitch hiking. Probably not, but it worked all by itself this time. Diane was a great short ride and left me with a genuine hug for the road. Good People.

She dropped me off at the last Sacramento northbound exit at around 6:30am. The only services there were dueling gas stations but luckily, while I was sitting on the station aisle making my new sign "REDDING PLEASE," a customer came up to me making small talk and offered me a ride.

Dave was on his monthly trip to Redding to see his kids. Decent guy, straight laced and buttoned down with deep republican views, that I of course was obliged to listen to. He wouldn't take any gas money and about three hours later dropped me at the Redding Denny's right off the highway.

It was brunch time and I hadn't eaten anything, just two cups of bad coffee from stops along the way. With my oversize pack and walking stick, I seemed to always turn heads, so I tried going into the restaurant carrying my pack over my shoulder with one arm. I still got sour faces from the employees, but not seeing a "seat yourself" sign I looked around for a booth with a wall plug and sat down. At first I was ignored. Not really ignored I guess, they all knew I was there, but service was slow and banter with the eventual server was curt. By now I was used to this treatment. It was beginning to roll off my back, so I made myself at home, plugged in all my electronics for charging and ordered water and a salad. The server's eye roll as he turned away was his first strike, by the time I left forty five minutes later he'd struck out several times over. Didn't think you'd get a tip? You were wrong, but oh so right. It's hard to imagine a dude with perforated earlobes hanging to his shoulders judging my choices. While eating lunch I got on my tablet and checked Redding out for my usual list of hotspots including thrift stores, natural grocers, shelters and parks. Redding, California turned out to be a beautiful place. Not too small, not too big, a wonderful setting in the lush Northern California woods. For my purposes it was just small enough to walk anywhere in town within about forty-five minutes, so I started walking. After perusing the town a bit, I once again felt a little empathy for the town and even my sour faced server. There were a lot of homeless folks, just like Santa Barbara and Goletta but worse. The setting was nice and even though I had no choice but to include myself in the throng of idle vagabonds, I decided to stay here and rest for a day or two. My first problem would be finding a place to stay. I was amazed but nobody seemed to mind. All the walkways, doorways, parks and wooded strips were already full of homeless hanging around so I thought down by the shore of the river would be OK. Turned out it wasn't when I started to get looks from the homeless folks camped there. I was obviously an unwelcome intruder. At least *they* could tell I wasn't one of them if no one else could. After awhile I walked past a road that trailed off into trees which had a hundred foot wide strip of wooded area on one side separating it from a commercial area with office buildings and parking lots. I walked a ways down that road looking into the trees and saw nothing but homeless encampments and trash. Moving further down, the road narrowed to country residential and a neighborhood watch sign had been placed conspicuously to warn off stragglers. On a hunch I kept going and found the woods after the sign to be clear of homeless evidence. My hunch was correct, there were no signs of encampments here. I broke through some bushes and was soon staking out a spot. Animal runs meandered throughout and it only took a minute or two to find a suitable place. Since the road was fifty feet away on one side and busy commercial office buildings not much further on the other, I needed a spot that was hidden from both. I came upon a little cleared area behind some bushes which was also under an overhang next to a medium sized tree. The ground next to the tree had been cleared of loam down to dirt and roots as if someone had purposefully made a little resting place. All the twig and loam had been pushed up against the bottom of the tree. I figured it was made and abandoned by another traveler, perhaps a conscientious type similar to myself. Since nothing was left there to hold the spot I plopped down and claimed it as my temporary home. The cleared spot was perfect size for my pad and bedroll. I unpacked most of my stuff from my pack and laid it conveniently around. Again feeling safe in my location I headed off to the nearby grocery leaving my stuff there hidden away in the brambles. No one would think twice about me walking around without my pack. I got back thirty minutes later with a couple beers and some snacks. It was about an hour before sundown and after a beer and a little reading I was starting to doze off when I heard some scratching and peeping fairly close to me. A little scared, I turned around slowly to find four turkey chicks just a few feet from me with mommas and toms not far behind. I studied them, they studied me. Neither of us were scared more than curious and they soon wandered off. Yeah, pretty cool.

I had a bit more trail mix, finished my other beer and started to read, but again fell asleep in the middle. It turned out to be four hours later when I woke to another sound nearby. My eyes opened to pitch darkness. I was hearing something slowly walking and scratching around very close to me. I lay there deathly still, trying to decipher the sounds. It sounded like a small dog but I could tell by the sound that it was going about its business not caring about me lying there.

This time I was a little scared. Wild animals will get testy when confronted and I was in its territory, I was the intruder and I could hardly see. After laying there still and listening for a minute, its meandering moved away, then back again, and then I thought I could hear it messing with my pack. This I couldn't stand for, so I quickly reached for my flashlight, turned to the animal and flooded it with 250 lumens of LED intensity.

What I saw there as both of our eyes adjusted to the bright light curdled my blood. A skunk was barely four feet from me, rooting through the loam.

As a dying man may see his life flash before his eyes, so too did the dire consequences of meeting a skunk in the woods flash through my mind in milliseconds. Primarily, no more rides for a month. I froze to subzero stillness and did the only thing I could think to do. In a tone as soothing as I could muster, with my asshole puckered tight, I started talking to it.

Weirdly, and I still can't figure why it was automatic, I was talking with a soothing French accent as if *I* was Pepe' le Pew.

> *"Hello Mr. Skunk, how are you? You sure are pretty, I luuuv you. Find anything good to eat? Be cool and I'll get you something from my pack."*

The skunks tail shot up with the tip bent over.

Mouth closed tight and eyes squinting tighter, I braced myself, vividly imagining and fully feeling the odiferous impact of what was surely coming next... but thankfully it never did. Mr. skunk never actually looked up at me or even stopped rooting around. He kept slowly moving, tail-up, seemingly ignoring me. He finally moved away and disappeared into the bushes giving me great relief. I thought he must be new at the spraying business. Perhaps he had never sprayed before, I didn't smell even the lightest odor of skunk. Either he was new or my French Dr. Doolittle impression was spot on. I soon fell back asleep feeling like a master of the wild.

The next morning was spent exploring outdoor areas of Redding and enjoying the lush atmosphere. Back at camp in the afternoon I sat back, took a light nap and then did some more reading. I was sitting cross-legged on my mat in the same spot I'd been for the last day. All my gear was scattered around with a few things stacked up on the dirt pile against the tree I was under. I had to get up and "water the bushes," so I marked my page, closed the book and lightly tossed it on top of the dirt pile barely two feet away from me. Just as the book hit the ground, I leaned forward and out of the corner of my eye I saw the book jump up an inch or two after landing. This seemed weird, so I reached over to see what was up without thinking, and as I repeated the motion to see if it would happen again, the dirt under the book jumped up at least four inches.

This unknown made my hair stand on end and immediately I jumped up and backwards onto my feet. I stared at that spot for several minutes not moving at all. Then, picking up a nearby branch and hoping to prove it was a hallucination in some way, I tapped and prodded all around the book at that spot. THUMP, THUMP again the dirt jumped up. Needless to say I was freaked out and jumped back several feet.
Keeping my walking stick handy, I slowly started packing my stuff, all the while keeping one eye on that pile of dirt. I nearly left that book sitting right there on that dirt pile. My imagination ran wild and after I finished packing I stood there for several minutes examining the whole area.
There was no further movement and no clues around to what might be under there. I've since come to the conclusion, either I was resting in a nest of some sort or by happenstance there just happened to be a ground dweller tunneling through right at that time. I gathered up energy and planned a fast retreat path thinking I would prod the dirt till I found out what was under there, but after another minute decided to let it be. After all, it could be a bed of snakes, a skunk den, honey badger or even worse, an entity yet undiscovered. The identity of which would only serve to vex those who eventually found my decomposing, half eaten body in the woods.

I walked away rattled but in one piece.

For several days following I revisited the whole situation, nurturing an attitude of survival. Grizzly Adams I am not, but enduring the unknown once again gave me another small boost of confidence in my journey. (*7)
Yeah! Grizzly Adams Jr. ... *jockin' the wilderness.*
From there I moved about fifty feet closer to the homeless encampment areas and soon found another adequate spot. Again, I hid my pack away and left the spot to find Wi-Fi. It was time to think about moving on. I needed to contact my next over-night sponsor in Mt. Shasta.
About forty-five minutes later it felt as though it must be a certain special time of day. Transient types had suddenly hit the streets, they were out mulling around like the walking dead. I had to sit on a corner curb for a few minutes and go a different way back to my spot to keep any of them from seeing me. As I was trudging through the weeds approaching my pack I realized someone had caught sight of me from next to the dumpsters in the commercial parking lot about fifty feet away. This person was looking straight at me, but it wasn't a drone from inside one of the buildings. It was a woman, a homeless woman, and she began meandering towards the trees in my direction. I sat down quickly on a fallen tree, but in a minute I heard twigs snapping and there was no doubt that she was coming over to find me.

"Hey Man !! where you at?! ...It's Cool... I'm Cool!"

It's not my practice to approach potentially negative situations in fear but I did make sure my most lethal utility knife was handy. I'm all about, "be as ready as a free person can be, don't run away, and just let things happen." I've found that rarely do new situations turn out the way our imaginations render. There aren't as many homeless women on the streets as men, I imagine them tougher. I expected a deranged psycho bitch randomly mumbling about nothing. Probably with the business end of a broken bottle in her pocket. She broke through the underbrush and stooped, then sat down not far from me on a piece of the same tree.

> *"Hey, what's up? Where you from? You smoke? You got a smoke? I could sure use a smoke, a butt if you got one."*

Brenda was a little tweaked. She wore jeans with thermals poking out from underneath. Three or more layers of shirts padded her torso of which the outer was a plaid wool men's lumberjack. Red high-top sneakers, purple Jansport book-bag stuffed to the gills and from the root growth on her peroxide colored, straw-like hair, it had been about six months since she'd last taken care of herself. From the moment she sat, I was being sized up.

> *"Don't smoke huh? What about anything else? Got anything else? Got any weed? ...any speed?"*

We sat around for a bit and smoked the last piece of the Wendy's cup bud pitched at me in Sacramento.

She was probably forty-ish and aside from her craggled and semi-toothless smile, you could tell that at one point she had been a beautiful woman... but those days were gone.

Right now, Brenda is a meth whore.

> *"You know... I know where I can get us a couple hits for thirty dollars. Its not too far."*

I gave her my standard answer by presenting myself as just like herself, homeless with no means, but she knew this wasn't true. She said that she had to meet a friend who was also going to get a few hits, but wanted to come back later. According to her, she really liked to "party" when zipped up on speed.
She got up and turned to go, then turned back around stooping closer to me while reaching out for my leg.

> *"Or... if you want... I'll suck you off for thirty.*
> *You've got to wash it off first though...*
> *I've got some water."*

So it went from hello, to blowing me in about thirty minutes. Almost a record for me if I'd have taken her up on her offer, but I didn't.
She took off soon after my rejection and I left shortly after. I couldn't risk her actually coming back later.
I walked toward the highway and spent the night between some nice thick cover bushes and a hotel sign. I don't know why, but outside in the fresh air, tucked away, I sleep like a baby. The next morning I raided the dumpster at the Shell gas station next door and

produced the proper cardboard for some good sturdy signs. "MT. SHASTA PLEASE," and "HAVE GAS MONEY," were todays lottery choices. After about two hours, a pickup truck pulled up and Jesus (hey-zoos) offered me a ride twenty miles to his exit.

"Almost to Lake Shasta," he said.
"Any services there?" I asked.
"Oh, yeah, A store, two RV parks, the cement plant where I work... a lot of stuff" ...he said.

Jesus let me off at the exit where he went every day to work, near the intersection of Lamp Post and Crickets. Seven cars left that exit going North that morning, all of which passed me right on bye... ***Seven.***
That afternoon, after finding "the store" nearly a mile away, I stood there hitching and counted another *twelve* vehicles with drivers nurturing deeply rooted reasons to not pick me up. I had plenty of water and food. I had a few books and all the time in the world to read them. This exit was in the middle of the woods so it was simple to pick a spot along the fence at the North bound ramp for the evening. Close to the on-ramp was OK, after-all, there wouldn't be any traffic noise. Looking back, nights like these were some of the best nights of my trip. Tucked away in the woods, there was a wondrous full moon in the sky that night.
No worries for tomorrow, it will all happen.
And tomorrow, it did. About 9:30am a semi-truck came up the on-ramp on the other side taking a load to the cement plant.

A little over an hour later, in this same truck, Gerald was turning his now empty rig North and readily stopped to give me a ride. This was my first ride ever in a big rig.

I asked him everything about the truck and his job and he told me all about it. He ran local Cali routes, taking old used tires to different EPA certified incinerators which were then used to power nearby factories, such as the cement plant. He said that he could take me to Oregon if I wanted. He was going all the way to Medford, but Mt. Shasta, California was my stop so that's where he left me. Unfortunately I left my rain jacket in the cab of his truck, and wouldn't you know, it soon started to rain.

Looking first through thrift shops and then the only other choice for a store with adequate quality stock, I ended up buying a new rain shell jacket at a local mountain outfitter shop. Fairly expensive but very good quality, Patagonia brand is worth it. Paying big money for a rain shell jacket will stick in my mind, I wont be losing this one anytime soon.

Mt. Shasta is a very cool and somewhat Metaphysical town. My friend Melanie lives there and had just birthed a baby the month before. The baby girl was magnificent (I love babies). Melanie lived in a shared situation but one roommate was out so I was able to get my pad down. We had a nice visit during the day and then a nice dinner. I hope to see Melanie, Baby Beauty and Baby Daddy again.

Maybe we'll reconnect down at my home base in Arizona where I met her to begin with. Good friends. The next morning I made it to the Burger King by the highway by 7am where I sat and had coffee. "EUGENE," and "HAVE GAS MONEY," were my signs of choice. After three hours of hitching directly in front of Burger King, I went inside again. There were several homeless folks around and many of them were inside the restaurant hanging out. The ones inside had money for coffee, the ones outside didn't. Outside they were mulling around looking scraggly and standing there talking with me. This was effectively "Busting my Hustle," so I went in for coffee and to check through rideshare listings on my tablet.
Inside I shared the place with a few legit customers and five others. There was an older guy named Bill going around talking to the stragglers and he eventually found his way to me. It took him a few minutes but soon I was recruited. Bill was the local Mt. Shasta Homeless Advocate. He went around to these people and many others daily making sure they had enough food to eat, warm clothes and a place to stay at night when it got cold. As a volunteer, he was a very good example for local governments and churches on how to get together to help the disadvantaged. After convincing him I wasn't in need of his services I left with him and helped him move a couple homeless guys belongings from here to there, then we took another guy that had sprained his leg to a local safe house.

For my help he would drop me off in the town of Weed, twenty miles North.
Deal and Done.
I've been to Weed, California a couple times. Once, like many curious travelers, as a tourist pulling off the highway because of the novelty of the name, (I still have a "WEED Police" tee shirt back in Arizona)
Another time visiting a friend that lived here and the last time I stopped bye to see the devastation left by the forest fire in 2014 that took out large sections of the town. The friend of mine, Steve, used to live there in Weed but his property was burned out in the forest fire. He was insured, got paid and got out. Now, in a different way, I'm here to get out too.
This exit on the highway consisted of four Businesses. A McGreasys, a Burger King, a regular gas station and a Truck-Stop type gas station with big-rig parking out back. The road into Weed from there was still closed off at that time due to the previous fire damage. If you got off the highway there, you must get back on the highway from there. It seemed like the perfect chauffer trap but it wasn't. I spent the rest of the day trying to hitch in front of the northbound on-ramp. In spite of hundreds of cars passing, no bites. About two hours before sundown, I went into Mickey's and used their Wi-Fi. I sent a few rideshare messages and re-filled my pack bladder.
Down the blocked off road, a ways into town, past the road barriers, the edges were growing back from the

burn. There were bigger trees that hadn't died from the fire and sparse scrub growth eight foot tall in areas. A tree about eighty feet off the road in a scrub field looked promising as a camp spot. Since more rain was nearly upon me I headed there to the shelter of its boughs. I had to traverse a dirt mound on my way and from its top could see a tent and small cleared area about fifty feet to the left of the tree. It was a nice quality tent too. I don't carry a tent. I use a 10'-12' tarp, 10 ABS plastic stakes, 25ft. of thin nylon line and a handful of mini bungees. All this is about the same weight but much bigger when opened-up than a regular one man tent. My tarp also folds up to almost nothing and fits perfectly in a pocket inside the main compartment of my pack.

The large tree needed clearing underneath. After a little arranging, I started to get my spot ready but soon was interrupted by crunching footsteps behind me. I turned to see my neighbor and his Pit-Bull walking up and he did not look happy. This dude was the dreadlocked version of Jeremiah Johnson with a two-foot pile of matted hair and threadbare clothing thickly layered (*8). He told me in no uncertain terms that he did not want me there. I should pack up and go and be sure to leave his stuff alone.

I tried to reason with him and was able to pacify him with small talk and praise for his dog. He soon calmed down a bit and walked away, though I felt it wasn't the end. My tarp-tent was up, strung from lower branches and I was inside opening my pack when he showed up again.

> *"You're gonna have to move maaan. I can't have you here fuckin' with my stuff. You're too close, I don't want my dog aggravated. You gotta go maaan."*

He was nervously doing a little two-step vibrational dance and seemed pretty agitated. I was a little concerned considering I had to be here till morning, I thought maybe I really should go. I wouldn't get any sleep at all if I had to worry about his manic state all night. All I could think to do was de-escalate, so I concentrated on a series of slow, deep breaths and explained my situation trying to be as nice and unthreatening as possible.

> "You don't have to worry about me. I'm just here till my ride comes to pick me up in the morning.
> I'll be out by five in the morning. Promise.
> This is the best place for being out of the rain, you know it. And if anyone starts fucking with yours or my stuff, you don't worry about that, I'll take care of that shit. I can't have that shit either man.
> I got somethin' for that.
> Don't worry, I got that."

A little solidarity and calmness helped bring him around. That, and a quick transition into the role of his protector. I gave him a couple trail mix bars and promised I wasn't leaving my tent till morning. That's the last I saw of Rasta Johnson.

He mentioned that he liked my tarp and thought it was a good one, so the next morning when leaving, I left him my tarp. I can easily get another next time I'm close to a hardware store.

When I got back to the truck stop by the highway there was a girl at the end of the building. She was leaned over wearing a black hoody, sitting on the curb smoking and appeared to be sobbing. She wasn't typical homeless with her small pink book-bag, stretch pants, high-tops and shock of bleached hair covering her eyes half the time. It was still before 6am, McNoodles wasn't even open yet so I went into the truck stop for coffee. A rideshare was meeting me there sometime around seven. A guy on his way through was going get off the highway and in his words, "*swoop me up*" on his way to Medford, Oregon. I had two potential stayovers with friends a little further North in Eugene, Oregon but a message received on my phone while sleeping nixed one. It turned out we were going to miss each other by a couple days. The other stay over was still up in the air, but a realization had come to me in the night, the upcoming Sunday was Fathers Day. A day I would like to be in Seattle to spend with my kids. I don't really look the part, but I'm kind of a softy. I was thinking about my kids and then saw this teenager sobbing at a truck stop, so I went down there and sat down next to her to see if there was any way I could help.

Turned out, LeAnn wasn't a teenager. She was 29, from Idaho, and trying to get back there. She'd started in South Texas and had just been put out of a big rig for not putting out. She was down and rattled with very little money left so I bought her breakfast at McDevils when it opened. She'd been on the road four days going back to Idaho, it was real easy for her to get a ride but nearly every guy started coming on to her right away. Some, like the last trucker, got really mean about being turned down.
I off-handedly imagined a role reversal there for myself. You know, like hitching was real easy for me because all the women wanted to pick me up and have sex with me. I wonder if I'd feel the same?
That's the light side. A darker thought is that she's lucky she hadn't been raped and thrown in the woods. Even myself having only one good arm, it would take quite an effort, for even the likes of an Amazon woman, to rape and throw me in the woods. But LeAnn's five-foot frame was easy weight for an average sized man.

There was room, so in a "under the wing" fashion, I had her come with me when the rideshare arrived. Weed to Medford isn't all that far and we spent most of the ride talking about piddley stuff. When we got there I topped of the gas tank of Steve's SUV which more than covered the two of us riding.
I'd been thinking about my timeline and realized the hitching had to be put on hold. It was too hit-and-miss. I needed to be in Seattle in two days, so we sat in a

Shari's diner style restaurant for a couple hours drinking coffee and perusing the rideshare listings. Although deeply engrained in the modern internet lifestyle, LeAnn hadn't yet heard of Craigslist rideshare. I think it might have ended up being her godsend.
If it actually happened, it looked like my next ride would be to Portland, Oregon in the morning. By 4pm we'd walked a little and I'd made a decision. I thought then, and I think now about the reasoning for that decision. I come out clean. I had even thought about a hotel before Seattle, pre-meeting LeAnn. So it was not an overt innuendo to copulation. I got a hotel room to clean up, decompress and have a safe place to pitch a fall-over buzz. I could be fresh for a probable arrival in Seattle tomorrow to see my daughter with whom I'd be staying. So far this month, this was my only hotel room (San Francisco Hostile not included), and that's something I'd allotted for. Those are all my reasons and excuses. I made no offers and with a big hug she immediately left to find her own way from there.
I must admit a deep worry about her right then though. It felt like I was feeding her to the wolves.
My room was on the second level and that night I looked out to my limited view of the road in front of the building a couple times wondering how she was. After a little time in the motel bar I ended up shit faced that evening, and for me, that almost always assures an early rise. When awake, I looked out my window a few more times.

Free Wi-Fi was another reason for the overnight room. My next rideshare confirmed for 10am, picking me up right out front. *Score.*

That would get me to Portland and then Seattle had to be a cakewalk from there in this environmentally conscious rideshare environment. I had already spent time looking through the rideshare listings and it looked promising.

It was early, five thirty or so, and I could still feel a little swerve from the night before. Down to baby carrots and a Cliff Bar, I went to the restaurant next door for a light breakfast. Within a few minutes of sitting down, two hands wrapped around my head and covered my eyes... *"Guess Who."*

I could guess, and was relieved to see her.

According to her, she had a couple offers that night but they were "scumbags" so she decided to wait around and see if I'd show for breakfast. I had promised her breakfast if she was still around in the morning.

We ate and then I offered to let her use my room to cleanup and sleep till my ride came. I promised I'd be gone until 9am. When I got back to the room, she was asleep but woke quickly. We sat around getting ready to leave and did a little dab I still had tucked away. Both of us being a little more open and receptive from the wake-n'-bake, she asked if she could tag along on my upcoming ride.

"Sure, as long as there's room," is all I could say.

I was non-chelant about it when she asked but she just

mentioned it before me that's all. I had decided I would take her to Seattle with me anyway. I can't be looking for that uniquely crooked smile on milk cartons the rest of my life.

I've gotta have some sort of closure here.

The rideshare worked out perfectly. Cool chick named Shannon. I wish I was ten years younger (I often say to myself). She was actually relieved to have a surprise woman passenger on the ride. She was afraid I would be creepy. We all had a laugh when I confided that was my fear of her as well.

Ha!... imagine that... Me...

Portland was typically dreary that day. Shannon dropped us off at her exit where we started to walk for a few minutes then sat down at a concrete picnic table in front of a Korean nail salon. It was a bit late and the only thing I could think to do in mind of my schedule was to head to the Greyhound Station. Several tries at CL rideshare had fizzled and hitching was still too iffy so we headed towards the Greyhound station. Luckily the distance was walkable within an hour or so. Along that walk LeAnn and I talked and I was surprised to find that in many ways she was quite insightful.

As we often find, but never seem to remember, a persons looks can be deceiving. I met several people along my trip that proved this observation to be true. I initially had LeAnn pegged as a "lost girl" but I was wrong. She was more like myself, someone wary from life's trials and just trying to get by.

I think back on that walking conversation to this day. I'm glad I met LeAnn, she's another person I encountered along my path who has changed my perception... if only just a little.

We had very cheap tickets to Olympia, red eye tickets. While LeAnn and I were talking about destinations and costs, a lady standing in line gave us the scoop,

> *"It's only $3 to Seattle from Olympia on city bus, aint no sense in Greyhound to Seattle from Oly. Save $20, stay by me, I'll show ya hows it go's."*

We followed her onto the sparse Greyhound bus in the middle of the night headed to Olympia. She opted for a seat up front while we kept moving to the un-occupied rear section. We were lucky to get the hop-skip bus in the middle of the night, and even luckier there weren't too many folks getting on. The next bus, arriving two hours later, was on a more direct route and would be full. I plopped my pack and stick down on a seat of their own in front of me. LeAnn slumped down within the added space of the rear seats and with her hoody wadded for a pillow, laid her head in my lap. The bus was on the road and the cabin was dark. Our talk soon turned, and within a few minutes there was a decision to be made. My choice was somewhat predictable, "just let things happen."
I'd been in this exact position long ago in the back of an interstate bus. There was nothing to do but sit back in a flood of déjà vu.

A Curb Caste Experience

Chapter Four

You can never go Home

In Olympia, LeAnn and I hung around and had breakfast. She was a bit more touchy, I was a bit more touchy. It was like a giddy beginning, but I didn't want to find out. Yes I did...Over and over again... Yes, but not really.
Our Public transportation oracle was correct. We got on a packed city bus to Seattle for $3 each.
LeAnn drug her hand along the handrail pointing to an empty seat for me and continued to the back to find her own. I struggled to remove my pack and smiled at the older lady in the window seat, she looked back at me with stern intent.

" No, no. ...uh, uh. this one taken," she shoo'd me off.

At that point, a very nice guy two seats back, cleared his three bags away and made me a seat. Nobody was standing yet but the only seat left was the one being held by Grandma. At the next stop a few blocks away a young woman with a baby got on. She walked past the open seat with Grandmas hand on it, and all the way to the back, but ended up coming forward again after

finding no open seats. She stood there struggling with the weight of the baby and asked Grandma about the seat but even she, holding a baby, was declined.
The bus was approaching the next stop and I figured to give up my seat but several folks got off, a few got on, the lady with the baby got a seat and lo and behold there was someone in the seat next to Grandma. She let her hand up for a young black man that got off two stops later and never looked twice at her. As soon as he left, she held the seat again.
After a few stops like this I started trying to figure out the angle from which her actions stemmed. Whether she was saving the seat only for black people or that she didn't want people of other ethnicities sitting next to her. I think it was that she wanted to make sure black folks got a seat. It seemed to me, in a weird quirk of circumstance, Rosa Parks was getting a small amount of reparation.
It was around 8:30am and looking outside, the traffic was a dreary sight. The bus moved along slowly but at least it was moving. All to be seen outside the bus lane through the windows was a gridlocked sea of cars. All lanes, exits and entrance ramps seemed completely packed to the limit. It was bad when I left six years earlier but I don't remember it ever being like this.

I think traffic has become a constant obstacle in our lives that is hard to overcome for most people. It has become our lives baseline and must be accounted for in all of our daily movements.

Wasting minutes here and there, hours in a week, and eventual days of our lives are wasted on traffic and the vehicles involved. Uhg.

I was checking out the schedule on the bus ceiling and noticed I didn't need to go all the way into downtown Seattle. Three stops from now would leave me under the highway at the West Seattle bridge, exactly where I wanted to be. I thought for a moment and dug a twenty out of my pocket. When the stop came up, I stood early and made my way back to LeAnn,

> "This is where I have to get off. My daughter lives in West Seattle. You be careful with yourself.
> Thank You for our time, I'm so glad to know you.
> You got the rest of this, don't forget rideshare and call me if you need."

She nodded and stood, I hugged her tight, kissed her forehead and forced the money and my card into her hand. It was hard to pull off that bandage.
I often wonder what happened with LeAnn. Would she ever by happenstance read this? She wasn't helpless and I'm sure she got along. Sometime in the middle of the next night I got a call from an Eastern Washington phone number, which is where she should've been. In my half awake state I fumbled the phone and somehow disconnected.
I didn't call the number back. I keep thinking I should have called that number back.

Off the bus, it turned out this was Grandma's stop as well. She was standing next to the bus stop pulling a Kool from its soft pack. Top foil neatly opened and reclosed on one side she started smoking backhanded with a standing swagger just like the days of old, keepin' it real.
I imagined she and I thirty years ago.
Yeah... we were cool.

From where I stood, Google maps showed an industrial area walk across to West Seattle. I took my time and meandered under the West Seattle bridge, completely amazed at the complexity of some of the homeless... homes. Even more so that they were built out in the open and apparently sanctioned in some way. Several contained huge rooms made of tarps and fabric. All surrounded by lives recent scavenges. It was like Ali Baba's retreat down there, except set on asphalt in the middle of a parking area under the bridge. All told it was probably a three-mile walk to my daughters. Her couch was big enough to sleep on and she lives in a perfect area having everything needed for a comfortable city life just a few short blocks away. Thai Food, Tap Room and Doggy Daycare, what else do you need?
The day before arriving in Seattle I started to notice an itch on my legs and arms with a little rash. The first thing I did after getting settled was to go find out about the cause of this increasing itch. If it weren't for my daughter's confidence in the Seattle public transit

system, the visit would have been much more hectic. Especially when going to the doctor to find out about this itch business. Public transit makes traveling around in Seattle very easy.

Soon after walking into a neighborhood medical clinic, up popped my next hiccup. I found that my healthcare plan is only good in Arizona. Everywhere else I had to use the hospital emergency room.

Yay, healthcare.

So next I went to the emergency room at a local Hospital. Within an hour or so, the verdict was in. The doctor opened the door to the examining room, took a look at my rash, asked me questions about my recent past and stood back. "*SCABIES,*" she said.

She was real nice about it too... but kept her distance. She told me it was typical, easily treatable and after hearing of my journey, what could be expected when in close contact with the homeless. I got a prescription for a parasitic death cream that pulled $150 directly from my tightly clenched ass. Eight hours after application I was supposed to be safe from transmitting, so everyone I came in contact with later was safe. It was the ones I'd previously had contact with I was worried about, what about LeAnn! Oh my god. This diagnosis was also troubling because I now had to cancel with at least three sponsors on my route. I wouldn't be contagious but I would be very self-conscious of my rash and the insistent itch would most likely make people nervous.

How could I show up to a friends house covered in an itchy rash?
A very distasteful situation to say the least.

Frustration manifested a little bit when at my daughters looking through rideshare listings, I tapped too hard on my tablet and broke the screen. As negative luck would have it, the crack went through the internal plug and rendered the tablet unusable. After a few days of trial and error it went in the trash and my daughters boyfriend, being a techie, gave me a new, smaller and much sturdier Kindle tablet from his unused collection, a lifesaver.
While in the Seattle area, traffic seemed to be buzzing at all times everywhere I went. I asked my friends about it and none had noticed a big change in traffic. Was traffic and congestion really the same back when I lived here but my base was such that it was normal? It's definitely one of the reasons I left.
I saw my Son while there in Seattle and made loose plans for later in the year. I also looked up several old friends and had some good visits. I checked out a few old haunts like my last house on Mercer Island. It had been replaced with a lot hogging behemoth and nearly all the rest I saw of my previous existence was strangely and sadly, different.
Indeed, Home *is* Ephemeral.

I'd been looking through the Seattle area rideshare listings the entire time I was there and even earlier.

I'd been checking to see the prospects of getting out of Seattle heading east. They were good. I had my pick of several offers going to Spokane and further. I just missed out on what seemed like the ride of the century. A guy from Michigan was willed a class-A motor home from his parents estate. He was looking for someone to drive it from Seattle, back to Michigan, he paid all expenses. What a dream deal that sounded like.
But of course, it's all about schedule. If ours would have matched… I can only imagine that would have been great.
What I did get was a ride with a guy on a late Friday night pulling a non-stop all the way to Ohio. A perfect ride since my next planned stop and stay over would be in Des Moines, Iowa, exactly on his route. All he wanted was company to keep him awake and someone to drive while he slept. Valid Drivers License required. He was asking no compensation other than that. A qualified applicant would *also* be required to sleep and eat in the car to minimize off the road time. I fit the bill.
My daughter was worried for me and hesitant of this rideshare nonsense but cranked up her car after a month of hibernation to drive me twenty miles to the pick-up point. It was Friday night, ten PM and the roads and highways were packed with traffic. It made me tense, my feeling of need to leave this rolling phone booth society was palpable.
Travis seemed like a really good guy with a 40mpg Chevy, rearin' to go.

He was the kind of cross country traveler that surrounds himself with all kinds of snacks and might use a bottle to pee in if needed. Only stopping when absolutely necessary for fuel and maybe #2. There would be another person now so hopefully we would be making pit stops, if only on the side of the road. I was hesitant about taking one long ride to my next destination. I'd much rather have a couple shorter ones, a little walking, a little hitching, maybe a chance to stay the night out in the open...

There comes an addiction with this type of travel as a lifestyle. The anticipation of "the next" haunts some of us in many facets of our life. From our baser instincts of sex, to spiritual advancement, "next" is a small and easily attainable goal. This hitching and rideshare stuff has become that with me. The new people, and tangents from new experience feed the whole, and through all this, all facets are satisfied, from sex to spiritual advancement.

Then there was my Santa Barbara friend Leon's idea of hopping a freight train across the badlands. I'd been in the badlands during summer in the past, they aren't called "The Badlands" for nothing. When you're rolling down the highway across a barren stretch of terrain with the temperature outside over 100 and there are snow breaks on the side of the road ready for twenty-foot drifts... that's a hint of the badlands. Since a good ride came up, I played it safe and took the ride.

Hopefully I'll make up for it.
We breached the speed limit the entire way to Des Moines and got there PDQ (*9). We stopped for food and gas somewhere in the nether on a couple of occasions and I threw in one tankful of gas as a gesture of appreciation even though I *did* drive about half the time. At one gas stop in Montana we were herded and held up by a Native American event on horseback. That was pretty cool, they were traditionally dressed, headdresses and all. Not too far from Sturgis, South Dakota we stared at a forest fire off in the distance as we drove down the highway. Helicopters were going to and fro with huge buckets of water from a nearby lake or river. Another temporary wonder to observe.
At three AM Sunday morning, Travis was sleeping. We were twenty-six hours into the trip when I pulled up in front of the Central Iowa Shelter and Services for the Homeless building in downtown Des Moines. It was drizzling and a few folks were standing around out front under the buildings overhang. After saying my goodbyes and thanking Travis for the ride, I went in. Early in the intake process I disclosed the supposed state of my rash-like affliction and they denied me entrance until I gave them a note from a doctor stating my condition was not transmittable. They pointed me in the direction of the nearest Hospital. It turned out the nearest hospital was my Alma Mater, the very hospital where I was born. The walk was gloomy, I trudged twelve blocks in a drizzle Seattle would be

proud of. The good news was that the Emergency Room in Des Moines, Iowa at 4am on Sunday morning was not busy at all, actually more like the morgue. Even better news was that this doctor refuted the diagnosis of scabies and even showed me bright glossy pictures of the same rash on his computer screen. It was a standard textbook, poison Sumac/Ivy/Oak allergic reaction.

The angels were singing! a weight was lifted from my shoulders. This explained why the prescribed ointment of deadly consequence didn't seem to work and the rash actually got worse over the past week. I was spreading it by itching. It all made much more sense now. I was completely relieved that I hadn't actually exposed anyone to "scabies" before I detected it.

Back outside with a clean bill of health I decided to go see another shelter that wasn't too far away. The first one I was at actually looked pretty nice but who knows, maybe I'd like this one better, the reviews online where pretty good.

When I got there it was sun-up, the drizzle had stopped and light was streaming through the clouds. These were all the ingredients for a glorious beginning yet this place still looked rather bleak. Their intake criteria seemed slanted toward veterans. Was I a Veteran? Over and over, again and again... Yes, I'm a veteran. No big deal, I claim no hardship other than karmic from my time in the military, but yes, I am a veteran, enough already.

This place was for men only and had a greasy feeling to its look. After looking over their rules, it turned out my backpack and I would be separated, so I had to say no-thanks. I can't describe it exactly, the place had a kind of a mental hospital vibe. Their schedule seemed a bit too strict and there was an amount of chapel and prayer in the mix also. I understand the reasoning for all that, but it's not for me. Thinking back, this place had an atmosphere perfect for the focal point in a M. Night Shyamalan film. (*10)
Where the second shelter felt dark and clinical, the first felt bright and institutional. The atmosphere at the Iowa Shelter and Services building was wide open and bustling. Kind of like a minimum security prison, except for the part where you can come and go as you please. They offer three meals a day, physical and mental health services, vocational and employment services, and a place to stay for up to sixty days if needed. A modern computer room, thrift shop and canteen/foodstuffs are available. There's cable TV and movies as well as a very nice gardening program out back in a spacious courtyard. While I was there, several different businesses showed up to recruit workers for various jobs and projects in town. A Carnival manager even came to enlist a few into the carny life. I found this place to be the best I've seen at helping and managing the myriad of human issues that result in and from, homelessness. After the intake process, which included them holding onto my knives and

walking stick, I went inside and plopped my pack down on an extended aluminum picnic table. It was one of about a dozen in a very large room. The Men's and Women's dorms and facilities, separated by vending machines were on one side. It was all windows and a door to the outside courtyard on the other. Two separate TV rooms and a laundry were at the far end and closer to me on this end I was sitting were the kitchen facilities. This room was used for a dining room at meal times and a screw-off room for the "clients" at all other times.

[One of the rules:] *No sleeping until evening sleeping hours.* This included me, even though I was very low on the snooze-o-meter and could have curled up nicely on the floor in any available corner.

Oh, **[Another Rule:]** *No sleeping on the floor at any time.* This included at sleeping time. Something I did not know when I denied myself a place in line for a bed. At the time, I was only going to stay for a couple days and I thought my pack, mat and bag would be great. Why take a bed from somebody that needed one when I'm happy with my stuff? **[Rules:]** *That's why.* Bed overflow "sleep" in metal armchairs in the TV rooms.

A statement as ridiculous as trying to sleep in an industrial metal armchair.

Entwined in my pack, I was sitting on the bench napping on the picnic table. It wasn't long before a room monitor noticed me nodding and came over to tap my shoulder after giving me enough time,

scientifically measured to be exactly before entering REM sleep, to remind me of **[The Rules:]**.
This gave an opportunity for my first new shelter friend to come over and sit down sporting an armful of colorful empty plastic bags and a folded up pull-cart.

> *"Hi I'm Mary, What's your name? What are you doing here?* (given no time to answer) *I'm not going out today, I'm afraid it's going to rain some more, besides its Sunday, I forgot."*

She was talking pretty fast, and in somewhat of a scripted manner. It was as though she was doing a bad Greta Garbo impression with her long chestnut brown hair and bangs painstakingly brushed straight. Mary was probably in her early sixties, wore pajama bottoms most days, was obsessed with the idea of sex and was a bonafide bag lady.
Without hesitation, she continued...

> *"See that man over there?* (she pointed at a crowd of people outside) *I saw him last Wednesday over on Euclid. We were over by the motel there. He tried to get me to go into a room with him and have sex. He probably heard I did that before. I didn't go with him but I should have. I'd have given him the ride of his life if you know what I mean.* (she gave me a set of googly eyes and a brush-off like she was a hot starlet) *You'll be next, watch and see, I know your type sailor."*

We had a few minutes of "Babs & Newman" type banter before she moved on (*11). In the end, Mary was always great fun to talk to. She loved to tell you who she wanted to have sex with and who she imagined wanted to have sex with her like it was the greatest of gossip at the checkout aisle.

It turned out to be a fine sunny day in the high seventies and was the last day of the Des Moines art festival just a block or two away in the downtown city park. After hearing about the local art event, I did what any self-respecting bum would do at 11am on a Sunday. I Grabbed my pack and left the shelter, perused the stalls at the art fair for a bit, found the beer vendors, a grassy knoll, and woke up around 5pm.

I was in Des Moines uninvited with no road sponsor. Specifically, I was there to see my Grandfather, my Mothers Father. If you do the math, he's in his 98th year. He is the only one left in Iowa on my Moms side besides a few distant second cousins I rarely saw when young. Even though first thought is different, Gramps is no worry, even at his age. He keeps passing his bi-yearly driving test and runs ahead to open the door for you. Not to impress anyone, no, because that's just the way he is and *he can*. He really is a marvel but I wanted to see how he was getting along right now. His second wife was in a bad way and it had to be taking a toll on him. I wanted to see if he needed any help. I'd be glad to stay for a while.

Betty, his wife, is a terrific lady and we love each other dearly but it was too much for me to stay with them so I happily spent my time there in Des Moines at the shelter. There was a very nice and sprawling city park not too far from Gramps' and I even considered pitching my tarp and staying there, but after all, the shelter *did* have three free meals a day.

While there at the shelter, I spent time reading, pulling weeds in the gardens and hanging out with a very strange brew. I also got to study and interact with a cross section of curb level Americans who seemingly represented hundreds of individual reasons for living at the bottom.

For instance, there is weeping Larry that carries around a sopping handkerchief all day. His eyes won't stop watering due to some sort of previous exposure to hazardous chemicals. Just talking with him made me tear up. Mimi is a dwarf. With her diminutive size and even smaller voice, she could be the sister of the dwarf actor in the old Clint Eastwood Western "High Plains Drifter." Christine sits at one of the aluminum picnic tables and rolls cigarettes all day from a huge sack of tobacco then sells them to others for .50c each. Business is better towards the end of the month, by that time everyone that has a monthly stipend is running low. Apparently she found that end of the month scrounged money buys cigarettes, a great niche. Christine doesn't smoke cigarettes herself but being a very large woman, in excess of 300lbs, apparently she does eat. All the money she makes on cigarettes goes directly to her pimp Little Debbie (just a guess). Walter stands in one place next to the TV room door all day, shifting weight from one foot to the other. He holds his oversize shorts up with one hand and picks his nose constantly with the other. I thought about talking to him one time to hear what his story was but he reeks of urine. Whenever the TV room door opens, the air rushes past Walter and into the room making the entire room smell like a piss pot. You don't hear the loudly squeaking hinges of the door as it opens, you hear the moans and pleas from inside the room to shut the door fast. Then there was Malik. Malik had been doing all he could to further the homeless stereotype by playing the free ride game and the staff were wary of him. He would do the minimum to get by and stay the full sixty days then leave for a month and come back for another sixty day stint. He seemed to be the stereo-typical homeless vagrant type but was actually the exception in this crowd.

Many folks at the shelter were infirm either mentally or physically but many were just in the depths of hard times and couldn't or didn't want to find their way out. Folks like Jumo and Glathia. Glathia was a traveler like myself but under much different circumstances. She had been on the road for four years and knew the best places in the country to hang out. She could no longer bring herself to live in a house or even an apartment. She'd been this way ever since she lost her husband, both children and everything she owned in a house fire while working the night shift at a packing plant in Arkansas. Jumo, the blackest skinned man I have ever seen, had undergone a "simple" elective surgery only to awaken to life in a wheelchair. Now, five years later, his life is spent in angst, fuming over his inability to exact retribution on those he saw to blame. This man is extremely bright and very capable, even from a wheelchair, I was actually amazed, but in my own condition I know the depths of his pain. His story gives me pause for the frailty of humanity.

There were many, many sad stories, too many to recount, but it seemed all had a common thread to which they clung. It's only my limited two-week observation of this crowd of course, but it seemed that most of them there felt powerless in their lives and could see no future. It seemed their only happiness came at others expense. Unfortunately, there was glee in drama and excitement over the pain of others. A very sad situation to behold.

The city bus was close to the shelter and cheap to ride so getting back and forth to Gramps' place was pretty easy. It didn't go directly by his place so I had to walk about a mile each time I went but I welcomed this bit of exercise and time to reflect. I'd think back to my childhood there in Des Moines and try to remember places that looked old enough to have been around for forty plus years. Along these walks there was one thing in particular that struck me hard.

A bit of déjà vu that was stronger than normal. It took me back to when I was a little boy. There must be a certain mix of flora and fauna in this mid-west town because the smell of the air triggered memories I hadn't recalled in over thirty five years, it was wondrous, I could remember the smell of the air. I hadn't smelled that exact mix since I was a little boy, right there in Des Moines.

Whenever I visit Gramps, he always wants to go look at the old haunts. I'm amazed at how many places I remember from back then that are still there. After-all, I was merely nine when my family moved away. The Des Moines population hasn't really grown very much since I was young either. The differences now being that when I remember those days, all the cars are 50's and 60's era and its in black and white. Back then, "Tijuana Taxi" was department store muzak and a dollars worth of candy was so much it could make you throw-up.

Aaah, the good-ole-days... so long ago, it really is like an old black and white movie to me. I still love Eames Era styling and that's what Des Moines, Iowa is to me, Eames Era. That's not quite how Des Moines Chamber of Commerce wants it portrayed. Judging by the billboards and downtown construction, they would like Des Moines to be seen as a cutting edge destination, but to me, in my little boy heart, it will always be Eames Era.

By the time I was ready to leave town, Gramps had me convinced all was under control so I left him on the monthly calling schedule.
Rides were not jumping out at me. I resorted to placing a "Ride Wanted" ad in the Craigslist rideshare section. Two days later I was very close to walking out of town hitching when I got a text from a trucker in Minnesota answering my ad. I called him back within minutes. He was on the road just over the Iowa state line as we spoke and was moving fast. I was walking around the downtown area at the time so needed to get back to the shelter. There were only two hours to get all my stuff together, walk to the bus, get on the bus for thirty minutes then walk two miles to meet him at the prescribed exit... I did all that... except.

These conniving muthers tried to steal my walking stick !

My pack was loaded up, I hefted it up to the front desk to get my knives and walking stick. When I get there, I look up and my stick is not there. My stick had been in the same spot for more than a week. Most of the staff people I was talking to at that exact moment knew about the stick and whose stick it was. Many people had commented on the stick. I just had them re-hang my name on the leather strap two days earlier. But no, now I get, "*what stick do you mean?*"
We found my knives after ten minutes, in the depths of their bucket system, and I was just about to change my tone when my walking stick finally showed up missing the leather lanyard strap.

The stick had been supposedly "found," in the corner of their break room. What was really happening was that it was being staged for a disappearance and I was lucky enough to catch it just in time. Any further along in the theft cycle and I would have had to cancel my ride and call the cops. I made sure they knew, in no uncertain terms, that stick was staying with me. I dreamt it up, searched it out it and cut it just right. I've been using it and watching it change color as it dries along the way. That stick had turned into my walkin' buddy and you don't leave your walkin' buddy behind.
I now had my stick back but it felt funny holding it with no lanyard. Thievin' fuckers.
Too bad, I had a real good review written up for their website.

I got to the truck stop twenty minutes late. We'd been texting back-and-forth so everything was cool, he was already there and waiting.
Peering ahead while walking, I actually saw the truck sitting there in the truck stop parking lot from two blocks away, it couldn't be missed. As I approached, I was all smiles and waved like a fool,.
I couldn't help myself. The paint job on the truck was perfect, even better than I imagined.

It was Bright Yellow and it had Flames.

A Curb Caste Experience

Chapter Five

Yes, it's True

I saw him see me from a distance and raised my walking stick in acknowledgment. He waved me up as I approached and I struggled to get my pack up into the cab where I found him talking on the phone. I got my stuff stowed and sat there till he finished.
"Yer him huh... Got any pot?" were his very first words. He was looking me over, sizing me up. I did not have any pot at that time, but I did share in the sentiment. As he drove, he got on his phone and called everyone he knew in the tri-state area to score some weed. This may seem like a tall statement but its not. Jerry was Southwest Iowa Alumni. Iowa, Nebraska, Missouri, this was the "tri-state area." We had a full load of paper for Wal-Mart in a dilapidated trailer on its last ride to the Mexican border. We had the fourth of July coming up and two extra days in the middle before this trailer full of paper had to be at the Wal-Mart depot warehouse outside Opelousas, Louisiana.
Apparently, Jerry's plan was to pick up some random traveler dude, pitch a flaming binge for two days then haul ass down to Louisiana to deliver the paper to

Wally just-in-time either with the remnants of the binge buzz or the actual binge buzz still in force. This seemed doable to me, put me down for a "*YES.*"

Jerry and I are really just two peas in a different pod. We have the same mid-west linage. Both of us have an Irish-Saxon build with the same mental cunning. He had been in the slam on a few occasions, once for an extended stay. I avoided the slam on several occasions with extended out time. He drove a fully loaded Peterbuilt like it was a toy, with little more thought than chewing a piece of gum.
I have driven a car.
Listening to his stories over the next few days I found that we shared many similar ideas about life. Many of the differences between us were primarily in the decisions we made, having had many similar circumstances. A self-proclaimed Outlaw Trucker, Jerry is either legitimately in the renegade faction of highway marauders or... he was trying waaay too hard.
Heading south out of Des Moines on U.S. 35 was just fine for a while but while futzing with his phone he discovered that a Department of Transportation (DOT) weigh station ahead was open.
He wasn't concerned that the truck was overweight because it wasn't. He was sure the most he could be smacked for was a couple trailer tire violations and maybe a light bulb out. After his paper drop-off in Louisiana the trailer was going to Mexico to finish the rest of its days.

Jerry said the Department of Transportation officers always fucked with him and usually detained him because of his extensive previous criminal record.

> *"If we go through there, I bet they make us sit 4 hours for sure. They might even unload me trying to find somethin'. There's a pike around this scale but I'll bet they got DOT patrols waiting there with portables for guys like me.*
> *Problem for them bastards is... I'm goin' cattycorner."*

After a while listening to his stories, I kinda started wondering if there actually *was* somethin' to "find." Jerry was telling me he was sure his movements had been monitored. They probably thought he was trafficking in something illicit. Tracking devices, cell phone taps and undercover agents were all part of this drama. I was hearing all this while winding through the Iowa countryside at 80mph on a county road, seriously no wider than two normal cars. There was no-one else around, this black ribbon was ours alone. As we freight trained along it was kind of exhilarating but all I could think was, "Big things crash Big."
We slowed down to fifty or so a couple times but just to go over go over a few deteriorating concrete country bridges. Some of these bridges were really old with no railing and a nearly missing curb. The concrete was crumbling away from the re-bar skeleton and you could see completely through in several places. They were simply decaying, no doubt aided by years of farm fertilizing chemicals.

But we weren't in an old lightweight farm pick-up truck. These small bridges most likely had a weight limit somewhere around twenty thousand pounds when built way back in the 1930's, 40's? We were at least double that weight for sure and the bridges are eroded in 2016 to a point where they will now barely hold a well-worded prayer.

In renegade trucker science; the faster you go over the decaying bridge, the less weight it feels. Our speed to weight ratio was way off, but about 50mph seemed to be a number that worked for the first couple of run-down bridges.

There was another bridge speeding toward us also. It shared its extremely dilapidated condition with the others but had the distinction of being just one vehicle wide and eighty feet long. In my shattered memory, which trades with nightmare, this bridge has a voice and a persona. It did not want us to cross it. Its entrance was like entering the mouth of an angry clown. With see-thru potholes and an I-beam overhang, there was no vehicle maximum height or weight sign to be seen. We were tooling along and crested a hill and – Boom- there it was. It was coming up quick and Jer' was trying to slow down quicker. I was watching the cows watching us when suddenly I felt the trucks brakes grab. I saw the bridge and saw Jerry's face as he gauged the height. I wasn't scared if he wasn't, and *he* was. I looked again at the bridge and still we were going too fast to stop before reaching it.

About a hundred feet before the bridge threshold Jer' let out an even tone, *"Oh Shit,"* and in the seconds following I was in a slow-motion vertigo. It felt as if life came down to only two choices at that moment. It was either the other side of the black veil or the other side of this bridge.

I imagined the roof of the truck being peeled back from the overhang and us falling through the bridge simultaneously. The truck would be dangling precariously from the bridge, our fate controlled by the maniacal clown bridge itself. I'd be destroyed, limply hanging out the window, flames licking at my body, clown bridge cackling.

"Aah Fuck it," gears gnashed, the engine spooled-up and the truck accelerated. Just as we crossed the threshold at 40mph accelerating, I glanced over at Jerry. He was looking up at the overhang as it rushed towards the windshield. I saw him give a sigh, *"we're good up top."*

The rest was a fog as the choice got closer.

Sitting that high off the ground, the bridge was like a bouncing crunchy cage rushing at us. I looked out to the rear view mirror to see the bridge jumping and swaying behind us. The gorge it crossed was forty feet deep and seemed to be swaying as well. I gripped the armrest and closed my eyes as the end approached. The choice had been made. After some very violent pothole bashing, we finally popped out the other side, unscathed.

Jerry was stoic and quickly got back up to speed. My mind returned from the fog and I took a few deep breaths to catch up on those I'd lost. It took several minutes to get over the sense of impending death, but it eventually left. I couldn't help but think that there are people that would pay big money for the feeling of complete apoplexy I had just experienced.
Can't bottle this, its gone.

While barreling down the road, we talked a little about our exe's and our kids. He wanted to stop at the next Wal-Mart and buy a few things to drop off at his exe's house. Hopefully she would be working her job at a local bar tonight and we'd go have a good time. At Wal-Mart I got a few things like a new tarp to replace the one I left for Rasta Johnson in Weed. Jer' got over a hundred dollars worth of foodstuffs and a new cell phone on the local monopolized cell carrier. I'd already found that my own Verizon system cell phone didn't work at all anywhere in Southwest Iowa or Northwest Missouri and his was spotty at best.
We got to the little town where his ex and daughter lived and pulled up in front of the house on a narrow residential street. Getting in there was quite an iffy thing and leaving was no better but Jer' drove that 60ft rig like sissy's Toyota. He did have to do some fancy jockeying around a few corners but he didn't bend a blade of grass on anyone's lawn. First, or second time either. We said our hellos to his ex, quickly unloaded the goods and scooted out before someone on the

narrow town streets complained. Then, half way out of town Jerry realized the new phone he bought was in a shopping bag on his exe's kitchen table.
Second time through, we continued on, Plan B was in effect. It turned out Jerry's ex wasn't working at the bar that night. From there we continued on to Rockport, Missouri, right across the line from Hamburg, Iowa. With good cell phone reception on his new phone Jerry was able to get hold of a friend in Hamburg. The only person that ever reached out to him when he was spending hard time in the can, a good friend. This was plan "B" because the results of proceeding in this direction had the potential to be much darker than if we merely got wasted and rowdied-up some semi-legal country bar. Jerry had come into Missouri on purpose. If we got caught for showing our asses in Iowa, his rig would be safely parked at this truck-stop in Missouri. We chatted up a few of the local "ladies," and halved a twelve pack before Jerry's friend showed up with his woman and newborn in tow. It was easy to see, Jerry's friend was zipped up on meth. After the introductions, I sat in the small car's back seat staring at the baby next to me. I was thinking about how far away I was from waking up this morning at the homeless shelter in Des Moines.
Poor, lovely little baby.
When we got back to Hamburg, we first went to the absolute filthiest house inhabited by humans I've ever been in. We were to meet another friend there.

I'll stop here and tell you that when I was a teenager, a poor friend of mine in Georgia lived in a singlewide mobile home trailer in the woods that was tipping into a sink hole. There was also a big, jagged, six-foot hole rotted through the living room floor. The hole was where their dogs and cats entered and left. We had to negotiate around the hole and garbage at the houses obtuse slant just to move about the "house."

Here, at this house in Hamburg, with the pitch of the floor urging anyone walking down the hall towards a brown room with a flickering light, I can't help but think this house was worse. Of course it had the requisite "fight-ready" Pit-bull, six cats, desiccated food, empty food containers everywhere... and there was worse but, nuff said. I pulled the sleeves of my overshirt over my hands as to not actually touch anything and stood breathing through my nose the entire time. I imagined something in the air entering my mouth to later develop into a strain of disease that would make bleach cower.

We stayed there till the expected someone didn't show up then went just a few blocks away to another good friends house. During the next night and day I met quite a few folks. It would suffice to say the following day would be all about brothers, sisters, cousins and friends doing drugs, a lot of drugs. We got a lot more beer, more pot was on its way and other things were already there. This house was equally as filthy and disheveled, but for a few added reasons than

the previous. People were pacing, everyone chain-smoked and the contents of the house were being spirited away for cash. Jerry disappeared a few times in the following hours only to return a short time later with a cleaning addiction. Over the course of sixteen hours and several bumps he literally cleaned-up half of this very large craftsman era house. Most of the time while there I sat in an old wingback chair pushed into a corner of the living room. I alternated between watching the zombies meander around the house and some bad programming on a fairly large flat screen TV. For some reason the size of the TV was deemed unacceptable but plans for a much larger TV were in the making, so I guess that will take care of something. Around two in the morning an unusual pair showed up at the front door. Donna and Marilyn had come over to deliver a bit of dope and to root through the house for knickknacks. Both were bigger, toothless women, who supposedly were much larger before their meth addictions took hold.
There's one for the tweaker plus column... diet plan.

The woman to whom this house belonged was in an elderly care center just a few blocks away while her meth addicted family sold the contents to their string of friends for drug maintenance.
I was asked several times over the next day if I wanted a bump but declined each time, opting instead for the next step down. Pot and alcohol were good enough for me, though maybe in a bit too overzealous a manner.

I did get ripped out of the socket that night, and for this, as everyone knows, we must pay the toll... in the morning. Except there really was no morning, not in the traditional sense, just a continuation of the same on the inside of the house as the day got on outside as a dreary, drizzly lightness. There was no way I was going to sleep with zombies meandering all around me. I thought to make some strong coffee but after looking around the house, I couldn't bring myself to use anything in *that* kitchen. I made myself the snack runner, took a few orders and I wired up on a lot of really bad coffee from the only gas station convenience store in town, just down the street.

Before Jerry and I were able to mooch a ride back to the truck sometime late in the afternoon, I sat on the front porch and considered my surroundings.

What were the common denominators here? It was obvious from my standpoint, and everyone I met that night had agreed. Hamburg, Iowa is not only home to Orville Redenbacher, the popcorn capital of the Midwest, it is also a never sleepy, little meth addict den in southwest Iowa. All of these people skeeved for money all day to get high by night and no-one and I mean NO-ONE was even close to happy. Normal mode of conversation contained nothing but negative topics. Also, everyone, including Jerry, either had false teeth or no teeth at all. If you were a meth head with rotten meth mouth in Hamburg you were a lightweight, this crowd was old school.

They had already been through their sober rehab periods where they had gotten their crumbling meth teeth pulled.
It's real strange when everyone around you has no teeth. It's all lisping speech and chins smacking noses.

After snagging a ride back to the truck, we were soon back on the road heading south, five brain cells short, and on-the-loose. It was on to St. Joseph, Missouri that night with a small scare about running out of fuel. Seems prices fluctuate wildly state-to-state and .04c per gallon adds up when buying over two hundred gallons of fuel at a time. St. Joe was going to be significantly cheaper but Jerry had never let the truck get this low on fuel before. One tank on "E" and the other just above made for a tense situation for a while. With my pack and stick ready, I was prepared to walk it out, but Jerry wasn't.
That night I slept outside the rig as agreed. I was in the bushes next to a hotel sign and slept well. Jerry didn't sleep very good in the trucks sleeper and was irritable the next morning. We'd brought beer, pot and probably dope with us so he went that route for the rest of the next day. The road was boring and all Jerry wanted to do was stay high and roust himself from crashing, both actually and figuratively.
At lunch I was happy for a change of pace. We pulled off the highway somewhere in southern Missouri and I was able to mark an entry off my bucket list.

When I was a kid, my family would occasionally travel the highways on vacations and other trips. On these excursions I would often see billboards along the road advertising "Stuckeys" and their signature, world famous, infamously luscious and delightfully delectable pecan logs. Yes, that's a lot of adjectives. A lot because that's all the Stuckeys pecan log was to me, adjectives. It was a marketing game. Every billboard we passed would use a different adjective in exciting print when describing the log.
I'd never had one of these treats, my parents had always denied me. I had so many glowing descriptions of this fine piece of confection in my head to which so much advertising along the highways had been dedicated that I imagined much. This had to be one helluva pecan log. I'd never had one... and here we were at a Stuckeys for lunch.

DRUM ROLL FOR THE PECAN LOG PLEASE...... eh, ok that's enough. Entry exxed off. Where's the trash can? I had that on my bucket list?... ick.

We rolled into Opelousas, Louisiana around three in the afternoon. Jerry was wired and tired and was starting to get on my nerves so I said my good-byes and hit the road.
Thanks Jer, it was... fun.
I made a "LAFAYETTE" sign and after just ten minutes standing at the head of the on-ramp, was picked up by Leon in a beat-up old Chevy pickup.

He told me he was only going ten miles, but ahead were all big busy interchanges from there to Lafayette with plenty of traffic so I could easily continue. I was kind of surprised because Leon was a young black dude. Within my life's extensive experience, it's rather unusual for a young black guy to pick up an older white man hitch hiking in the Deep South, I would not have guessed it. He was a regular good guy and made my heart feel good. He was in the process of rolling a blunt on the fold-down center armrest but needed some help finishing, pot crumbles were everywhere. I got in and he started driving down the road but was disappointed to hear that my right arm now precludes me from rolling joints... blunts too.

> *"Ok, that's cool then, I'll just do what I was gonna do in the first place."*

He immediately pulled off the side of the busy highway and finished rolling the blunt. Leon was on his way home from work and wanted to get his head straight before getting there. His woman didn't like him smoking pot around his baby.

The cops did not roll up behind us on the side of the highway like I had imagined and we drove another ten miles getting bent. It was pretty good stuff too, I just don't like blunts very much. Mixing it with tobacco paper and flavors is just too harsh for me.

Leon let me off at his exit and I stood there about an hour, thumb out, before an old eighties station wagon pulled up with smoke rolling out from underneath. I looked in the open front passenger window to talk with the driver but smoke choked me out and made me wince.

> *"Aah, don't worry bout' that. It's just an oil leak, it doesn't come in when I'm driving... you ok?"*

I caught my breath, quickly pitched my pack in the backseat and got in so we could start the car moving, letting the smoke waft behind us. The ride wasn't long to Lafayette from there, maybe fifteen minutes.
My new driver Jameson, a great chauffer name, let me in on the recent and on-going adventures of his self proclaimed "coon-ass," Louisiana family then left me off at the I-10 East / West exit coming out of Lafayette around 6:30pm. This was just enough time to get along and find a good spot for the night. I was able to find a nice set of bushes in the back corner of an empty lot next to a gas station which worked fine. The extra environmental traffic noise of the area didn't affect me at all, I slept great.
Not homeless... Bedless without a care.

A Curb Caste Experience

Chapter Six

South of the Border

I spent quite a bit of time in the South when I was young. Georgia, South Carolina, Alabama, I stomped all over those grounds and made a nuisance of myself in a few other southern states as well. Although I had two invites from folks in Georgia and one in Tennessee, I hadn't planned on going there because the southern states, or perhaps I should say "the things I've done in these southern states," has always left a bad taste in my mouth. I wanted to traverse the next couple of states as fast as possible before landing in middle Florida to see my Mom and Siblings.
Like all good holidays that depend on a date for their name, the fourth of July fell on July 4th this year, easy to remember. Like most big boisterous holidays, everything and everybody, stopped to enjoy. Although I was ready to keep going, no-one else was. There were no rideshares going from, or through, Lafayette that day but fortunately I was able to set up a ride with a guy coming through from Dallas to Baton Rouge the following day. I walked downtown and spent the rest of the day checking out the city before enjoying a good

holiday meal and the 4th of July fireworks show at sundown. It was a pretty good day but I had a long walk back to the highway area to sleep. Along the way back, at the Lafayette Visitors Center, I found a large clump of bushes that had previously been hollowed out in the middle for my sleeping pleasure. I was able to lye back comfortably and see the remaining fireworks from my new nest.

Yes, once again, very comfortable.

Morning travel breakfast at McGlommys and Wi-Fi to check-up and make sure of my next ride was just in time. I woke, packed, walked and had just enough time to eat and cleanup before he showed up.

Exactly on time, Raymond came through like a cool breeze and picked me up in his new, bright red Chevy Spark. Originally from Detroit, Raymond liked the South but he didn't like the heat. The A/C was on full blast the entire time and was actually kind of uncomfortable, it wasn't terribly hot outside yet. It's only a little over an hour to Baton Rouge so I survived without putting on a coat and had him drop me off at a downtown exit. I was in Baton Rouge for a day and a half. While there walking around I sat to take a rest at a bus stop. I laid my pack and stick against the overhang and was holding a conversation with a nice lady waiting for the bus. Within a few minutes more people showed up and noticing more room was needed I looked to my pack to scoot it between my legs and noticed something missing.

I quickly turned to the lady I was talking with and asked her to watch my bag then jumped up and looked all around. There was my walking stick in the hands of a scruffy dude walking away quickly. He must have felt my gaze because he sped up to a jog. There really was no match. He wasn't far enough away and not near fast enough, even at my age, I can run like hell. When he looked back and saw me within twenty feet, my stick fell from his grip and he took off running. I got my stick back but looking to the bus stop, people were boarding the bus. I instantly imagined my pack gone now too and made it back to find the nice lady gripping my pack waiting. I thanked her with a hug and paid her bus fare then sat back down clutching my stuff. Sometimes it's just not worth the hassle of owning something nice. That night was the night of the 2016 Baton Rouge cop killings. When I heard about this, I forgot all about rideshare and hitching. I thought it best to move along in a timely fashion so I got to the Greyhound station and headed to Florida by bus.

Tallahassee, Florida was next, the stage for several of my teenage scenes of iniquity. I lived many of my teenage years in an area right over the Georgia border from Tallahassee and we would come to the "Big City" on occasion to have a wild time. Even worse was Spring Break not far away in Panama City Beach. Those were the days of drinking age adjustment. When I turned eighteen, the drinking age was eighteen. That same year the age went to nineteen in Georgia but I was "grandfathered in." The same thing happened when the age turned twenty one. I was on the good side of the cusp. Back in those days the drinking age in South Georgia was just a formality anyway. All it meant was that you could walk in to a legal bar. Even then, a person was rarely carded if they looked remotely old enough. I'd been driving on public roads and buying beer in stores since I was thirteen. We were country boys and pretty much did whatever we wanted. Anyway...

I arrived in Tallahassee early in the morning around sunrise and resolved to walk from the Bus terminal in the downtown area to the furthest East I-10 on-ramp, then hitch the rest of the way to my Moms house from there. The day turned out to be quite hot so about six miles in, I found some nice grass under a broad tree along side the road and took a rest. The breeze blew through nicely and it was two hours later when a city lawn maintenance worker woke me up so he could mow the area. The way those guys looked at me, I really felt like a homeless dude right then.

I'd walked twelve miles to the highway on-ramp and when I arrived, the last thing I wanted to do was to start hitching so I copped a squat in the only travelers restaurant at that exit, a Waffle House. There was one other restaurant there, tucked back aways and seemed to be very popular. I forget the name, something about food from the farm, my kind of premise. I've made a mental note for myself to go there if I'm ever in

Tallahassee again under different circumstances. For the time being, the Waffle house with its A/C and iced tea would have to do. I actually have a soft spot for the House of Waffle. I spent many a morning in the Waffle House as a teenager in that small South Georgia town I lived in, drinking coffee and smoking cigarettes. It's where I drank my first coffee and my last job in Georgia before leaving for Florida at nineteen was as a short order cook at that very Waffle House.

My back was aching from the days walk carrying the pack and my shoulders were killing me. I opted to find a place to unpack and relax for the rest of the day and then get on with it in the morning. This was a semi-wooded area so it wasn't hard to find a good spot not too far away.

After so many times unpacking for the evening it was easy to get my gear set-up. Soon everything that was needed for this length of stay was at arms reach, strategically placed all around me. I journaled and read, had an avocado and trail mix from my pack and fell asleep before dark. The next morning I had the road standard breakfast at Casa Waffle and raided the gas station dumpster next-door for a few pieces of good cardboard to be my next signs.

Lake City, Florida was only about a hundred miles East but it might as well have been a million. The previous night I'd vowed "*no excuses,*" to take the easy way out. I ***MUST*** hitch from here to my Mothers in Ocala, no matter what may come.

An early start would liken the chances of catching a ride from folks leaving the two hotels nearby. I stood at a very busy corner that led directly to the eastbound on-ramp holding two signs. "GOING HOME EAST," and "HAVE GAS MONEY," didn't work. Going home wasn't exactly the truth but I was going to see my Mom and most people consider where their mother lives as home, don't they? I kind of do, but it made no difference. By noon, way over a thousand cars said no to me in as many ways. The heat had gone up several notches and I was beginning to sweat while standing still, the heat wasn't so bad, I'm from Arizona after-all, but the humidity was brutal.
At lunch I went in to the Waffle House and chatted with the waitress for awhile. She was talkative and asked my story, fully expecting a sorrowful tale from the standpoint of being a homeless vagrant. She was surprised when I caught her up on my journey, it wasn't exactly what she expected. I declined her offer of a free meal and left a nice tip. Grilled cheese sandwiches at the Waffle House are common but Irene's compassion was certainly not. Before I explained to her that I put this all on myself and wasn't without resources, she was conniving ways to help. What a nice lady she was. She sent me back out to the road with a large cup of ice water and something nice to think about. Around two in the afternoon I was eying the gas station pumps behind me, thinking about enlisting the direct confrontation method, when I

heard a car horn blowing right behind me. Someone had pulled over to pick me up in a convertible and I didn't even notice.

Martin was 54 and retired Army. His high and tight hair, squared off chin and a fit appearance would make it easy to call him Sarge. His Mitsubishi Spyder was a slick ride and we got up the on-ramp and onto I-10 East in a flash. No sooner had we merged onto the highway when Martin reached down to the floorboard in front of him and pulled out a Busch Ice 40 ouncer. Already popped and half empty, he took a long swig and told me there were more if I wanted one. I thought for just a second... *might as well.*
What else could I do? If I get out and he goes on his way, I'm out a ride, and he's still drunk driving. At least this way other drivers on the road have me in this passenger seat to help guide us away from wrecking. Not much, but something. Besides, I understand drunk folks fare better than not in horrific car collisions. With no top on the car I could just pop my seatbelt like an ejector seat while we're flipping in mid air and likely land in the bushes mostly intact. Yes, I was a bit worried, but I played the game for hitch hiking's sake. How does the saying go? "Beggars can't be choosers." Martin had three more 40's in a bag in the back floorboard. I popped one for myself and he downed the rest of his asking for another. By his age and the way he kicked back beer like it was water, it was obvious he was no beginner.

More likely, he had graduated to the level of functioning alcoholic, and was driving ok... for now. He had no destination in mind and in the time it took to get to Lake City, recounted what turned out to be the most disturbing story of my entire summer trip.

Martin's wife had died four years earlier. They were married for thirty some years and loved each other at the end as much as the day they were married. She was a true gem but had developed a cancer. Her medical bills were tremendous and it was all they could do to pay the insurance deductibles from his Army retirement and his wives reduced pay at Wal-Mart where she had worked for seventeen years. She eventually took a turn for the worse, couldn't work at all, and by some "twist" was let go from Wal-Mart and her medical insurance canceled. A few months after her COBRA medical coverage ended they were bankrupt and it was at this point that his wife passed away. She lingered long enough without insurance for both of them to nurture a deep resentment for Wal-Mart and for her to pass on a way for him to strike back at the company for their callous treatment of her. Since his wife's death four years earlier, Martin had been trifling every Wal-Mart store he came across for hundreds, sometimes thousands of dollars per month. His wife had been a manager with a specialty at the service desk and knew all the angles. As I write this, I see on the internet that Wal-Mart knows of this scam and is now looking for ways to crack down.

When we got to Lake City he showed me how it was done. Well, not actually showed me, but after explaining the deal, he went into a Wal-Mart and came out with more money than he went in with, about $60 that time. Every day along the road, each town he came to, he would stop at every Wal-Mart and pull this scam. Sometimes to the tune of several hundred dollars a day. This is now what kept Martin alive, this is what kept him going. He was addicted to fucking up Wal-Mart's bottom line. He figured that was all there was left for him. He tried the gun barrel in the mouth method but found he couldn't pull the trigger and that made him feel worse. He was very distraught. Now four years later, he wept in a drunken stupor as he talked about his fallen wife.

After stopping for two more forty ouncers, a series of pee stops and then another round from the next gas station, I took the wheel and drove. I'd been pulling the old beer dumping game and hardly drank a full twenty ounces in total from the two cans I "finished." My driving gave Martin the chance to sleep a little and weep to himself about his situation. Since he had no destination, he wanted to give me a ride all the way to my Mothers place in Ocala so we took a right on I-75 South at Lake City, Florida and headed to Ocala.

In Gainesville, Florida while waiting for him in a Wal-Mart parking lot, I called my Mom and Sister informing them of my location and asking them to be ready to pick me up at the Ocala Wal-Mart parking lot in an hour or so when I texted them. I tried to think of ways to help Martin but it seemed too late. His situation had turned into an obsession, a true mental tic. When my Mom and Sister showed up at the Ocala Wal-Mart, I thanked him for such a long ride, wished him well and bid him good-bye.

I spent the next week at my Mothers, frumping around Ocala in a typical ho-hum "what's next?" fashion. The week after that, I moved across town to my Sisters for another weeks stay at her place. Everyone in my family works during the week, and the weekends are typically continuations of the last but what we were really waiting for while twiddling thumbs in Ocala was for my Brothers girlfriend in Tampa to have their baby. She was due, overdue actually, and we were all anxiously waiting. This would be my third, and hopefully last nephew. We're all getting a bit old for this, which makes a new baby even more exciting.
We all scooted to Tampa the weekend after she gave birth. After the initial welcoming visit, Mom and my Sister went back to Ocala and I stayed in Tampa at my Brothers house to help out.
Tampa, Florida is where I spent a few of my formidable years. I left that small town in South Georgia for Tampa right after my nineteenth birthday and left from Tampa to enter the Navy halfway through my twenty-second year. Hard to believe, but that was thirty-one years ago and I haven't been back since.

While at my Brothers I helped with the baby. I also helped him catch up on work he'd missed the week of the birth and checked out the town by foot and car as much as I could stand with such dense traffic and expanded population.
You may have noticed by now, I don't appreciate city dwelling. Ever since leaving Seattle in 2010 I've seriously de-compressed and try to multi-task as little as possible. Since then, visiting big cities starts to wear on me after a few days. I thought the traffic and mayhem was bad when I left back in the eighties but now the small City limits meld with the large City limits and the maze of highways have become much more intense. I wasn't able to recognize anything except the names of streets, I mean absolutely nothing. Even my old house on the river had an extensive makeover and was virtually unrecognizable from its earlier days. The strolls through the previous places I've lived serve to reinforce the idea that my actual home is *planet* Earth and all material things on this earth, including our homes are completely impermanent.

A Curb Caste Experience

Chapter Seven

The Back Half

I left from Tampa on a rainy Monday morning. From there on out, I was on the last half of my road trip, on my way back to Arizona. I still had no time limits or strict schedule to keep but was starting to reap the oats I'd sown. My left knee, was getting progressively more clickety since I took a light tumble down an embankment in Louisiana and turned it. I had recently been enjoying a respite and I didn't want to possibly aggravate it again just yet. I decided to purchase an unlimited Greyhound Bus ticket to Albuquerque, New Mexico, the town where my next road sponsor lived. An unlimited ticket lets you get off and stay at a stop on the route with no time limit to dictate when you must continue. This type of ticket costs over fifty percent more than the same on a direct route with no refunds, although if bought far enough in advance is still very cheap for the distance traveled. What lowered the cost even more was that I had picked the routes and times with the most stops so I would have the opportunity to hang out in more places along the way. My ticket was twelve stops long.

I could get off and stay at any one of these stops, or even jump ahead on foot and pick up later at a different stop further along on the route. Any place my knee said "no," I could simply continue by bus. A pretty good deal for a journey like mine if you can stand riding the bus, it can be trying at times.
First stop was Jacksonville, via Orlando and Daytona Beach, a swap over to the east coast. The bus ride was standard fare with a normal fifteen minute stop in Orlando. Once on our way again, about twenty minutes outside Daytona, the bus slowed down to around 40mph and wouldn't go any faster. There was a malfunction somewhere and the bus was hobbling into Daytona where they would hopefully get us on our way. It took awhile but we finally got to town, off the bus and sat around waiting for word. The word that eventually came was a lot more wait and while waiting I was able to check on the craigslist rideshare listings from Miami going north.
Raul texted me back within minutes and was out front of the bus stop in half an hour. He was on his way from Miami to Atlanta and needed gas money to do it. He had given two short rides already and one person was still with him in the car to eventually be dropped off later in St. Augustine. He answered my text while driving down the road and I had luckily messaged him just in time for him to swing by and pick me up. The drive with the three of us started out just fine. Jana, the other rider, had some powerful original strain Indica

with him that put me to sleep soon after he got out in St. Augustine.

It was probably the pot, Raul had smoked it heavily also. Possibly, it could have been that I was unclear or that Raul misunderstood somehow, but when I woke up a few hours later, the first thing I saw out the windshield was a road sign,

"**Georgia State Highway 23**"

We were nearly to Macon, Georgia.

Realization came quickly and I asked Raul why he didn't stop in Jacksonville. He was incredulous and started hitting me up for more gas money. This made me kind of angry at first, it felt as though I had been kidnapped for gas money, but with nothing else to do, I quickly formulated a new plan.

Damn. For many years I've been confidently spouting that I'd never go back to the state of Georgia under any circumstance. I should have known better than to say that, Never say Never... here I was.

Ten more dollars for gas shut Raul up but if he tried to squeeze any more I was going to start walking. I fake slept the rest of the way to Atlanta so I didn't have to continue arguing. At the last gas station in Podunk Center I called a friend outside Benton, Tennessee. I'd previously called Angela about a month back and told her I wasn't stopping bye, but now that my plans had changed she was still glad to hear from me. In fact she insisted on driving to Atlanta to pick me up. I met Angela while gold prospecting with friends in Montana

a few years back. She, and her then boyfriend Brandon, were part of a prospecting club that was there at the same time. Our crowds were camped together and we hit it off great. Angela still followed me on Facebook and when I posted about my upcoming trip, she offered her place to rest. Now, hearing of my debacle, she offered to pick me up at a Denny's in Marietta, Georgia where Raul was going. She was already there at the Denny's waiting when Raul dropped me off.
As I pulled my pack and stick out of the car he had the audacity to hit me up for gas money again.

> *"Hey man, you should leave me another ten for gas. I brought you right where you wanted to go."*

"Yeah, sure" was all I could muster as I walked away. He'd already gotten $25 from me for gas and another three to four hundred miles out of my way to boot. I originally put in money for a ride just over a hundred miles so you can suck on it Raul. It wasn't the money that was upsetting. It was the total disregard he had for me, taking me so far out of my way just so he could get what he wanted. Good-Bye.
Angela was inside drinking a hot chocolate, reading on her kindle, it was a great relief to see her. The trip to Tennessee seemed very short. I guess travel and a lot of talk is tiring because after we got back to her place and had a bit to eat, we were both asleep by 10pm.
Three days at Angela's place in the woods was very nice. She is a fantastic cook and a professional woodworker, I was amazed at her level of skill.

A very rare mix of beauty, brains and abilities, I could stick around there for a long time, maybe forever... but eventually the road calls.
On the fourth morning Angela insisted on taking me as far as possible. I was able to find a rideshare from Dalton, to Warner Robbins, Georgia. So Angela got me forty miles to Dalton by 9am to meet my ride.
Thank you Angela, you're fabulous.

My ride showed up just a few minutes after I was dropped off. Leonard was a musician (keyboards) temporarily staying in Nashville, now on his way home to Warner Robbins, Georgia for a few weeks with family. He was a very "hip," dude and very involved in himself. I thought it amazing that he even shares rides. I probably need to know more about him but one thing was for sure, the ride with him was a quick and easy trip through the maze of highways and traffic that is Atlanta.
In a greasy spoon diner in Warner Robbins I had my pack on the table with a sign propped up against it. "WEST OR SOUTH. HAVE GAS MONEY, THANKS." Several people walked bye noticing and sat down with their friends talking about the sign... and me. Eventually one guy that had been sitting at a booth in the corner since I came in got up to leave, paid for his meal, then walked over to me and started a light conversation asking about my journey. I wasn't impressed with his condescending look, but he did offer a ride in his own peculiar way,

"I'll give you a ride as long as you aren't a weirdo."

I was mistakenly sure I could win him over.

Jeff was going South on I-75 till he hit I-10 East and then on to Jacksonville. This meant I could soon be back to I-10 at Lake City, Florida. Jeff was a true redneck, born and raised. He had two guns in the truck "just in case," and wore a confederate flag belt buckle. He thought it was terrible the way folks nowadays disrespect the American way of life with all their gayness and drugs. Tree huggers should be tied to a tree to see how much they really love them, and God was saving us now from Obama. That's how he knew God was real. The only reason Obama hasn't turned us over to his Muslim brother "towel heads" was through Gods intervention. Go Trump.

Oh God, how about a little more intervention in this truck? ... the stuff I'll do for a ride.
I sat through the dissertations quietly not really paying attention but using my active listening skills with the occasional head nod and "uh huh."
It turned out Jeff had given me a ride to straighten me out. The green tie-dye, Grateful Dead tee shirt from the Oregon Country Fair I was wearing as an attention getter while hitching gave him the idea that I was in need of some common sense schooling. That's why he offered me a ride, to speak his mind. Apparently us tie-dye wearing liberals have been turning up everywhere. Some of us don't even have a car.

What kind of American is that?
Completely tense from a four-hour ride with a witch hunter and at last free, I put my thumb out at the Lake City I-10 West on-ramp. It was now fairly late by hitch hiking standards but the sun was still up so I decided to try my thumb for one hour before stumbling over in nearby bushes. Surprise of all surprises, my luck was on, I got a ride in about ten minutes.

Jen and Sheri were going to Tallahassee. They were very nervous about picking me up. Picking up a hitch hiker was an ultimate adventure for them and a way to indulge their imaginations. Think Thelma and Louise. (*12) Neither had ever picked up a hitch hiker before but being together gave them a feeling of solidarity that no head lopping highway murderer could withstand. They'd already loaded up with snacks before getting on the highway and we were "Rocking Out" loudly. Their enthusiasm and indulgent sizes taxed the front seats close to their limits. In reality, they were two of the most fun people to give me a ride during my entire trip. They were on their way to a paid seminar for their employer to learn more about their jobs. By their playful demeanor you'd think they were on a "let loose" trip to Las Vegas. The ride was just over an hour and we enjoyed each others company with laughter most of the way. They let me out at the same exact Tallahassee exit I had left from with Martin and his convertible a month earlier. Right after I pulled my pack out of the car, Jen, the passenger, grabbed me back from my goodbye hug and asked if I wanted to go have dinner. I could stay the night in their hotel room with them.

Under different circumstances I would have led the way, but in this particular situation I had to bow out. I still wonder how it would have turned out if I had gone that direction. I'd probably be slinking around in a smoking jacket right now with a big bushy mustache, low rent environmental music lightly playing around me wherever I go... chika-chicka-bow-wow.

I found the exact spot in the trees I had a month previous and it looked as though there had been no visitors. Soon sprawled out like I was at home, I slept like a baby.

The next morning I was lucky enough to get Irene as my waitress at the Waffle House. "Lucky?" Hell, she seated me at the head of her station. She was excited to see me again and was insistent, wanting to hear all about my travels since we last met. We excitedly talked about where I'd been and my Brothers new baby. I had a lot of pictures of the baby, did I mention I love babies? Especially my new little nephew.

After breakfast and another send-off, I donned my pack and walked across the gas station isles next door to get to the road. I had my new signs tucked under my arm while checking out a handful of motorcycles gassing up at the pumps. I'm an old motorcycle guy and appreciate cool bikes so I stepped closer looking at a Russian Ural motorcycle with a sidecar.

The owner came out of the store and we soon started chatting about his bike. Although relatively common, I had seen these Russian Ural bikes from afar but had never actually taken a close-up look. Mike was more than happy to show me his bike and introduce me to his friends with the other four bikes. All five were taking a long ride to Pensacola, 150 miles away, and were gassing up for the trip. One thing led to another and before long, Mike took his rucksack out of the car seat to wear, arranged my pack to fit, and I got my first ride in a motorcycle sidecar.

I know, that sounds fun, I thought so too. After all, how many folks get a chance to ride in a sidecar? Unfortunately at this point, I can't recommend it.

I was all-smiles for the first ten miles or so but it took a full two and a half days to de-vibrate from that short trip. We had to pull over once to fix the tie downs for my pack and when we stopped for gas again I almost called it quits. Although I was at wits end, we eventually made it to Pensacola in one solid piece. I was a bit grey when we finally stopped and Mike apologized again and again. That's when he told me that the vibration issue was why his wife hadn't come along. She was afraid riding two-up on a motorcycle so he bought the bike so they could ride together. Two short rides later, she couldn't handle the vibration. Turns out I was Mikes crash test dummy to verify his wife's complaints. He previously thought she was being whiney but I assured him she was a real trooper if she went more than twenty miles in *that* tin can. He vowed to have it checked out and we all parted company with a handshake not too far from the Pensacola Greyhound station.

The last time I left the ticketed bus route, my trip grew some beautifully crooked branches and everything turned out great. Those were fun and interesting convolutes to the trip but I now had the additional vibrational effects of my sidecar ride and my knee issue wasn't much better.

Pensacola was one of my ticketed stops so I decided to get off my feet and back on the road in semi-comfort. After Pensacola I rolled into Baton Rouge once more, which in turn after a short layover, became New Orleans. Things were moving too fast. The bus passed through Alabama and Mississippi in a blink. I didn't want to show up anywhere early, so I got off the bus in New Orleans. I had started to feel like a wounded road-war veteran with my vibration ghost, numb flat-ass from the bus seat and clickety knee issue. I did my best to shake it off and went sight seeing for a day.

That turned out to be a blasé decision at best.

I have been to New Orleans before, a couple times actually, and each time I can distinctly remember vowing to myself "never again."

But do I listen even to myself? No.

I'd been here twice pre-Katrina and once post Katrina, (Hurricane Katrina) and now this time I took inventory and tried to figure out why I chose to look again.

I decided that even though I enjoyed the idea of raucous partying, I was now past immersing myself in it for very long. I could no longer handle throngs of loud and gleeful inebriants. I could no longer handle drunken stumble bums showing me their mis-shapen and tattooed tits. And above all things... I've never been able to stomach New Orleans jazz. Banjo and accordion music set my teeth on edge. It hit me soon after "As the Saints come marching" played for the third time in twenty minutes.

The beads, the tits, the music... the indigestion.

I stayed at a Creole Inn that night and even the night desk manager's accent irked me. It wasn't them, it was me. After a short while I realized it was my "Ant Hill Syndrome," directing my thoughts.

I just have to be out in the open, that's all.

The next day I waited around the bus station till the next Westbound came through and continued through Louisiana and into Texas. Dallas has a fairly large Greyhound Station and it was packed. There, I was propositioned for sex *and* drugs... ...aaah, it took me back to the good ole' days.

Back in the late 1970's, early 80's when I would ride the bus as a teenager, I soon found out what kind of folks hung out at the bus station. Any bus station I'd ever been at was the same in that respect. There was always at least one dude peddling pot if not more. You had to be careful though, most would rip you off if you gave them a chance.

Even when I wasn't riding, I knew I could go down there and get pretty much anything I wanted.

While I was there in Dallas I started thinking about my friend Robert in Austin and thought to give him a call. When he didn't answer I left a message and thought to just get a ride and show up but since he hadn't heard from me in over a year I held off. Austin is a cool town, the white sheep of Texas. Thinking back, maybe I should have gone, but then again that would have changed the circumstances for everything that happened after Dallas and as it is, I'm happy with how my trip turned out, so...
The bus was packed tight from here on, things weren't as comfortable as I'd imagined they should be, and on top of that, the bus was having problems. It started outside of Wichita Falls where we had to pull over on the side of the road several times. This type of thing seemed the norm by now and since I didn't have immediate schedule, I didn't mind much. Besides, this bus full of people was quite a study. There was the usual type with their face in video screen, beeping away, including four people who wanted to get off the bus each time it stopped to hunt pokemon with their smart phones (WTF?). There was a group of belligerent twenty somethings loudly voicing sexual innuendo and worse to any woman or girl who glanced their way. And there was a group of five teenagers traveling together who proved to be a welcome respite from the other passengers.

These kids were dressed normally, talked to each other, played word games and not once did I notice any of them look at their phones or any other electronic device. It's a strange turn in my life that this behavior stands out as different.

We were three hours late into Amarillo where the driver threw up his hands announcing to the busload that this was his stop. We were supposed to get a different driver here but our bus was too broken to go on and there wasn't another available bus anywhere close enough. The Greyhound employees at the station did their best to get everyone on new buses to their destinations but there were still thirteen of us "stranded," in Amarillo.

Everyone else had a schedule to keep but I didn't. Everyone else felt stranded and complained incessantly, I didn't. Everyone else was quite upset about the situation, I wasn't. Of course I had a mindset to walk out of there but Greyhound was about to dole out reparations for our inconvenience and I wanted to be around for that. I had graciously let everyone else be taken care of first since I was in no hurry. Because of this, I and the other twelve passengers had to stay over till the next day when the next buses came through. We would then be re-seated as seats were available on any continuing bus. Sitting there for so long, I struck up a conversation and bantered for hours with a woman who was under similar circumstance.

Lindsey had a quick wit and a sharp tongue, she was heading south and had a snafu in her schedule. She arrived at the bus terminal the day before to an over-booked bus and was having to wait in the same fashion as us but she had fallen asleep on a bench in the terminal and missed her next bus. Her ticket was again advanced to the next day but she had to stay there waiting once more. She'd been in the bus terminal nearly three days and after watching business as usual in the depot, had developed a dim view of Greyhound. She was frazzled to say the least. It was early morning by now and Greyhound gave us thirteen stranded passengers, a meal and a hotel room for our troubles. We would all have to wait for the next bus to come through at 7pm the next evening.

When the hotel shuttle came to pick us up, it could only hold five at a time with luggage so I waited for the last trip. I decided to ask Lindsey if she wanted to cleanup at the hotel and get a real meal, on Greyhound's nickel. We had turned into fast friends and she was in need of some relaxation. I didn't know how to say it without it seeming like a "come on," because it kinda was, but I finally spit it out and she gratefully accepted with certain restrictions that she laid out playfully. I could tell by her tone and eye contact that she had similar ideas so we ended up letting things happen and enjoyed each others company till her bus came through that next afternoon at four.

In the meantime I'd been searching the rideshare listings from any town along I-40 that might have someone passing through Amarillo and before too long found one that clicked.

There was a listing posted going to Phoenix from Mississippi. All I needed was a ride to Albuquerque and I wasn't getting back on the bus. I considered myself waaay ahead considering the value of the meal and hotel Greyhound gave me was almost half of what I paid for my entire ticket. Never mind my new friend.

I'd gotten a hold of Jim, my next ride, in the morning. He had plans to stop in Amarillo around six for dinner. The deal was if I showed up at the Whataburger in Amarillo at six, he'd take me to Albuquerque for the cost of dinner and $20 gas. That didn't sound bad, I really had little choice. I wasn't getting back on the bus, my ass could no longer take the seats. Besides, I vowed never again... like that works.

I've cleaned up my act in my mid years, I try to eat healthier and eat less. I'm generally off fast food now and rarely step foot in these types of restaurants nowadays for a regular meal.

This aside, it's a dark secret now, and select few people know, but my true junk food gastronomic weakness is Whataburger.

Yes, that is sad, but if this Jim guy likes Whataburger then I like Jim. For me, Whataburger is in the same realm as the Stuckeys Pecan Log. It's a childhood wonderment in which I never got to partake.

Mel Tillis, the stuttering Country crooner was the Whataburger spokes person back in the 1970's, which made this place even more mysterious to me.

"WH-Wha-Wha wHaaaata burger!"

When I finally went to that much longed for fast food restaurant later in life, unlike the Stuckeys Pecan Log, I really liked it.

Jim was a little late which struck a worry chord, but eventually rolled in around 6:20 in a new, loud, flashy pick-up. We talked about the finer points of cars and Whataburger, he was all about cars. He was driving a pickup truck right now but had a few favorite cars back at his home in Mississippi. This is a topic I am very familiar with. In a previous chapter of my life, I was a professional mechanic with top of the line industry certifications.

Somehow, by the time we got to New Mexico, cars had turned into politics. I don't have much to say on the topic of politics so I was silent most of the time. I didn't care for his views and I knew if I voiced mine, I'd most likely be looking for another ride in short order. I held off including myself in the political conversation for as long as I could. A lot of my responses were merely a light "hmmm." I just needed to get within a few miles of Albuquerque so if I actually answered any of his questions or interjected some rational, unselfish thought, I'd be close enough to walk.

By the time we reached Santa Rosa, New Mexico, Jims tone had changed a little, he was starting to suspect he

was giving a ride to, as he put it, "a libtard."
"Discretion is the better part of valor," as the saying goes, but about ten miles outside Albuquerque, completely insane with trying to shut him up with silence and diversion, I cracked.

"It's strange no-one today calls themselves a Lincoln Republican,"

I led with, just to see if he new the comparison.

"What level of education do you have?"

Was the ramp for his ire, but I didn't go much further,

"That's just selfish to start with and fuzzy logic at best," was as pointed as I got.

After I started engaging in his conversation it wasn't long before Jim shut up completely. He didn't say anything else till he got off I-40 at the Fourth Street exit in downtown Albuquerque, pulled over and stated with finality,

"This is your exit"

"So I guess no ride to the doorstep?" I jeered him.
His answer was a cold stare and squealing tires speeding away towards the highway on-ramp.

{**Note to self:** *Finding that someone also likes Whataburger does not make them a kindred soul.*}

The four and a half hour drive left me in front of a Weck's diner style restaurant in downtown Albuquerque around eleven in the evening. The town was shut down, nothing within eyesight was open including the diner.

The friend I'd come to visit worked night shifts so wouldn't be of any help. I looked up her address on Google maps and kicked myself. She didn't actually live in Albuquerque, she lived eighteen miles north in Corrales. Jim and I had discussed this to start with, he was going to drive me to the house. That's where my snippy parting comment came from, as it was, I had a long walk ahead of me.
The first ten miles were directly north up Fourth Street. There was no use in trying to hitch, it was late. Even I wouldn't consider picking up a hitcher after dark. Besides, this wasn't a very good part of town. There were very few cars at this hour except the occasional thumping chrome sled and cop cars, all whizzing by like they had places to go in a hurry. With nose down and a one-hour rest stop in the middle, that part was behind me by 5AM. Next came some country residential side road trudging till I crossed the Rio Grande River at Alameda, New Mexico around 8am. I stopped there for breakfast at The Flying Star restaurant. A fantastic place tucked around the corner on the road to Corrales. Lynn was on her way home by then and when I got hold of her, I told her I was near. It had become a mission to finish this walk. After breakfast, the best part of this long walk began.

Horse trails through the trees along the Rio Grande irrigation waterway was a very nice stroll. I met over a dozen people along the way that were walking, biking and riding horses.

As I got closer to Lynn's house in Corrales it seemed that nearly everyone had horses on their property. I was enjoying meeting and saying hi to people. I was obviously a study for them with my huge backpack, steady pace and walking stick, not too many hikers through here I guess.

While resting for a minute with my pack off next to the trail, I was feeling very good. Approaching was another walker with a fast paced gait. I readied myself and smiled nicely while giving a happy "Good Morning." He looked up at me, and with a sternly contorted face replied,

"There's no Camping here," then quickly walked on.

I was stunned, crushed actually. What was that all about? Some folks just need a "wake n' bake," and apparently he was one of them.

The tree overhang on the trail kept me in the shade until the last mile and a half. From there I popped out into the open and finished the walk under a rising New Mexico sun. It was just before noon when I finally arrived and gave a slightly weary knock on the door.

I spent a week at Lynn's there in the Albuquerque area. We went to Santa Fe and Taos to hang out for a day but other than that, her place was very relaxing.

There was a choice. I could wait there in Corrales and in two weeks when Lynn's work contract was up she would be heading to my same oasis in Arizona to hang out. I could ride back with her, or I could continue on as I had been doing.

I wasn't quite ready to call it quits yet and wanted to go to Pie Town, New Mexico so I landed a ride out of town. Pick-up for my next ride was eighteen miles away at the exact Weck's restaurant where I was dropped the previous week in Albuquerque at the I-40 highway exit.

Ever since San Diego when my Uncle used the Uber public ride service I'd been curious about how it worked. He raved about it before he called for an Uber car to take him to the airport the day I left his place over two months ago. The morning of my departure I downloaded the Uber App on my phone, jumped through the hoops to get it up and running and caught an Uber to my pick-up point in Albuquerque by 9am. It was a good ride. On-time, quick and easy in a clean newer car with a smiley driver. It felt similar to catching a Craigslist rideshare except for the structured monetary rate involved, similar to a taxi, but for quite a bit less. The best part about this ride was that when you join Uber, the first ride is free.

I still tipped the driver though.

A Curb Caste Experience

Chapter Eight

Home Stretch

I arrived at the diner a little early. My next ride and I had only texted each other, we hadn't talked on the phone so I had no imagination of what he looked like from that perspective. As I walked through the front door I looked around the restaurant hoping to spot someone looking for me but... no luck. I sat down, ordered a light breakfast and played a game with myself. From only his style of writing, vocabulary and circumstance I wanted to see if I could pick out the correct person as customers came through the front door. I thought he would be mid twenties, thin and somewhat of a beatnik. The game was ruined when he texted me from the parking lot of his arrival. When Mark came through the door five minutes later, I found my mental picture of him was correct.
Mark was tall, mid-twenties and an aspiring fiction writer meandering his way to Portland, Oregon. After we sat and talked over breakfast he gave me a ride West on I-40 for about sixty miles until we got to the exit for state highway 117 heading south.
That road would take me to Pie Town.

I didn't mention it earlier but Pie Town, New Mexico was always in the plan. In fact, within the loose jumble I called a plan, it wasn't till after Pie Town that I could consider myself to be in the home stretch. I had come to know of this unique town from a segment on TV several years back and since then, have heard people talk about it. By the time I started hitching south it had become an obsession, but the sign I had stuck into the back of my pack read:

"PIE TOWN / QUEMADO - THANKS"

Quemado was a larger town further west I would go to only as an emergency alternative. I was effectively walking out into the desert, there would be seventy miles of nothing but scenery before I reached the next sign of civilization.

From the single gas station at that exit, I stocked up on water and headed south down highway 117 with my thumb out. I'd stretched out roughly five miles under foot with barely a dozen cars passing before Enrique pulled over to pick me up in his beat-up, loaded-down Chevy pickup. I had to share the passenger seat with his best friend. A quite large, super stinky, very happy, mutt dog named Chuay (a Mexican name, pronounced "chewy"). Also sharing the space was a large vintage metal cooler and what appeared to be a couple decades worth of trash. All of which kept me sitting on the front edge of the trucks bench seat. His girlfriend was following behind in her own car. Enrique was leading the way to a special place in the mountains where they would camp for a couple days and harvest a particular kind of moss for his landscaping business. He took me a few miles further than he was actually going and dropped me off at a recreation area that he figured might have better ride potential. A really nice guy, he offered me a six-pack of beer for the road. He had a lot of beer with him, several cases. I declined the whole six but did take two singles for emergency hydration purposes. As he drove away I felt an emergency throat fire coming on and luckily had means to quench the sparks. I needed to get them out of the way. After all, I wouldn't pick someone up hitching down the road drinking beer and I wouldn't expect anyone else to either. It would be hard enough on this stretch as it was. There wasn't a lot of traffic on this road and the skies were building dark clouds. After a couple more miles walking I decided to find a stand of trees that would support my tarp tent just in case I needed to spend a rainy night in the high desert. My shoulders were aching and it was time to take a rest. I found a suitable place next to a boundary fence, set up a few things just in case and was soon lightly nodding. About thirty minutes later I was stirred by a nearby rustling and other strange noises. I looked around and was enchanted to see over a dozen wild horses staring at me from about thirty feet away on the other side of the fence. They were all quite disturbed by my presence and the three colts with them also appeared spooked and worried as they pranced back and forth behind the herd. This meeting of nature in the desert was pretty cool and I felt privileged to find myself there visiting with these beautiful animals, but the clouds had lightened overhead so I packed up and quickly left so as not to bother them anymore.

On the road again I kept my eyes open for a good stand of trees to hide under in case it started to pour but every time I stopped to rest, the skies obliged and held off. Luckily the rain never caught up with me, but during the next stop when I almost fell asleep it would have if not for the chirp and drone-like hum of a Humming Bird friend.

I'm very familiar with Humming Birds. My Arizona Oasis is a yearly migratory stop for a variety of different species. When I left my place in Arizona there was a tiny humming bird nest on a branch just ten feet from my RV door. This little guy here was either waking me before it rained, urging me on, or was sore I was encroaching on his feeding haunts. I like to think that word got out in the animal kingdom that I was walking about and they were looking out for me.

A very satisfying thought.

After walking a few more miles and looking at the map on my phone I realized the road sign a hundred yards ahead was pointing south to Pie Town, and straight west to Quemado, this was my turn. From here I estimated about thirty more miles to go. I was deep in thought on the possibilities of my destination and failed to hear the Semi-truck coming up behind until its brakes squealed, slowing it down as it passed, pulling over to give me a lift. I quickly walked up to the trucks cab and jumped up to see the driver.

"Are you going left up ahead?
Are you going through Pie Town?"

"Naw, I'm going through Quemado"

"Sorry you stopped man. I'm going south up there ahead at the turnoff. I'm going to Pie Town."

I'd turned down my first ride and felt weird about it, especially out here in the middle of nowhere. I had imagined turning down rides, but in my imagination it was be because I opened a car door to find the driver with his dick in his hand or maybe a horrific smell or a driver covered in communicable lesions. Good honest, "no-one could stand that," reasons, but pie?
Turning down a ride for unknown pie?
Will it be hot? Will it be a la'mode? Will it even be good? What if this "Pie Town" is straight out of Sweeny Todd? At the very least, I'll hold off on a haircut till after I leave. (*13)
This trip to Pie Town better be worth it.

The driver shrugged and moved on with a wave, leaving me to what turned out to be a thirty-seven mile dirt road, Pie Town Rd. Seeing the name of the road on the "street" sign at the intersection gave me a fresh start. Pie Town must be a thriving place for them to name a long road like this after it.

Right then it felt like I had reached the head of the driveway leading to the house of nirvana. Unfortunately, it wasn't long before this giddy feeling of bliss was squelched. Within the first two or three miles there were a couple ranches and a few trucks going back and forth, after that there were no vehicles at all. Pie Town road sizzled through a barren stretch of desert for many, many miles.

I'd been walking Pie Town road for about two hours, singing a song similar to "Follow the Yellow Brick Road" but changing "Yellow Brick" to "Pie Town." I was a bit slaphappy and getting low on water.

Keeping an eye on the clouds and the sun, the clouds were not an issue now but dark would be here within a couple hours. The landscape was mostly scrub, with no trees to speak of on this stretch, so I was scouting cattle guard fence posts to use as a tent frame to drape over and snug down my tarp. I had been off the side of the road doing this when I heard a vehicle coming from the North. It was a big pick-up truck towing an RV trailer. As it got closer to me, the truck slowed and pulled to the side of the road. After exchanging niceties Stuart and Jim offered up a ride.

Yay! Stuart and Jim!!

These two were riding the road scouting possible Elk hunting grounds as they headed towards their hunting camp to the west of Pie Town. According to them, this was the best Elk hunting area in this part of New Mexico. They had already spotted a few.

Even on the brief drive from where they picked me up we saw two Elk, one with a huge rack of antlers, walking across the road ahead of us plain as can be, about a quarter mile away. These two were merely a couple of good guys out enjoying the American wilderness, and while they were at it, just happened to save me from the desolate tortures of Pie Town Road. This day, they were my favorite guys, Hell Yeah!!
A lot of hunting stories and testosterone laced talk later, sometime around dusk, they dropped me off in what I thought might be the outskirts of Pie Town, ... Aaah, finally, Pie Town.
Stuart and Jim let me out in front of a cluster of dilapidated buildings. One was an old gas station that had many of its windows broken out and was barely standing. I went in and looked around for a minute. Digging my flashlight out of my pack I could see the worthless remnants of not only the previous business but also the trash and destruction inflicted over the years by other people curious of this old building and its contents. There was rat rice everywhere and luckily the usable remnants of a broom. I swept up a large area then laid down my pack for the night. Although untested, it was a roof and by this time it was nearly dark. I went to sleep that night trying not to judge Pie Town. After all, what could I see in the shadows? At best, a few old buildings through what could turn out to be a very narrow perspective. I closed my eyes concentrating on finding a town of greatness waiting

for me in the morning and slept well.
I woke and packed up at sunrise, I wanted to get out in the open before anyone saw me emerging from the old gas station. Once out on the main road, I looked up and down the barren district realizing there really wasn't much there. By 7am I had figured out there were three pie establishments in town and not much else. The one I had seen featured on TV was only open certain days and times. Today was an "on" day but I'd have to wait till 11am for the doors to open. Another shop there was supposedly the best from what a few stragglers told me, but their open hours were erratic. The third was next to the Pie Town city administration building and was open regular restaurant hours. The Pie Town Administration building struck me as humorous. There can't be more than a hundred people that live here amongst the trees. I imagined one elected official inside at a desk next to a large hat rack. Fire down the road? He'd jump up and grab the fireman hat and a garden hose on his way out the door. Stray dog? The animal control hat. Someone speeding through town... the policeman's cap would get dusted off.
The pie shop next door was open for breakfast with a standard breakfast menu but the rest of the day served pie and coffee only. I went in chuckling about the imaginary hat rack and had pie and coffee for breakfast. This place was small and cozy, they baked their pies in a 6-inch size. I took a few minutes to peruse the pie case of many varieties but finally chose

a Blueberry with a butterscotch drizzle version. Do you want to hear all you need to know about Pie Town pie in three words?
It- was- divine.
A little much to eat at one sitting but carrying leftovers with me on the road wasn't an option. I ate it all. Besides it was great pie... greatness realized.
So in summation;
"No gas, no this, no that... pie... Pie Town."
That should be in big letters on the town water tower. I crossed-out PIE TOWN on my cardboard sign *and* on my bucket list before I left. (Is my bucket list sad or what?)
I walked off a lot of pie in the next two hours of stepping. This was old highway 60 and would eventually land me within twenty miles of my oasis, the real home stretch.
Right then, along the highway as I plodded west, I still had a couple hundred miles to go. Cars were passing me like roadside garbage but eventually a car stopped and gave me a lift.
Paul was taking his son Brian to the University in Phoenix. They had just passed me as I was walking, I saw them do a three-point turnaround in the road ahead of me and head back. Noticing their maneuver I imagined they had left something behind at the restaurant in Pie Town, but then they repeated the turn-around maneuver once past me again and stopped to pick me up.

It was quite an effort to stop for me, as they pulled up I was happily wary.
These two were not your typical ride givers. They were more thoughty and straight laced. I was thinking they had a bet going but I never figured what it might be on. They wanted to know about my trip like it was some type of research project or something. Sometime during the drive, the conversation took a turn to life philosophy. We jabbered on and waxed philosophical till Show Low, Arizona. They planned on taking the northeast route into Phoenix and I still needed to go a little south so they dropped me there in Show Low.
Now, this was the real Home Stretch. I was just three hours away and the remaining road was almost all downhill. Even though, I'd still be lucky to get all the way back to the oasis today. It was Saturday, mid afternoon, and the only trick I had left was hitching. There aren't any interstate buses that come through this area and Craigslist rideshare was empty in this neck of the woods. Not surprising since the areas around Show Low are mostly Apache Indian reservation and they try not to "follow the white man's ways" (good for them). After changing my pack sign to "GLOBE PLEASE," I started walking. After putting in a couple miles on a winding mountain road with no shoulder to walk on, a pick-up truck pulled over. Inside were two Native American guys and a dog. This was a regular cab truck so there was no room inside. The passenger told me they'd take me 25 miles to their

turnoff and gave me the motion to get in back. They waited while I lowered the tailgate and hefted myself up still wearing my pack, into the rear bed. Once the tailgate was up again I rested against the side with my pack as a cushion and my arm draped on the tailgate in a relaxed fashion. With a wave to the driver through the blacked out rear window, we took off.

I mentioned previously that the remainder of the trip was nearly all down hill. This next stretch also cuts straight through the White Mountain Apache Reservation. Being in this vicinity, these guys were probably White Mountain Apache, most likely on their way to Cibecue (Fort Apache). According to my phone map, the turn-off to Cibeque was roughly 25 miles away. We took off and in no time were whizzing along pretty fast. I didn't mind the speed so much as long as the driving wasn't erratic. This was an even grade, but eventually when we started going down hill and hugging the winding canyon road at over 60mph I started to get a bit worried. It was all I could do to hold on to the rail to keep from bouncing all over the truck bed. I tried to peer through the blacked out rear window at the driver, then to the passenger side wondering if there was a menacing or maniacal face staring back sadistically but could see nothing. The asphalt was a bit bumpy and the truck had a shake at certain speeds. Between this and a sudden swerve, my good hand's grip let loose from the rail and I started to pinball around the bed of the truck.

If it weren't for my thirty-five pound pack strapped to my back I would have been tossed out for sure. I was weightless many times as the truck pitched me up and bounced me against the rail time and time again. I felt like a turtle on its back being tossed and scooted around.

Quick snippets of paranoid thought started going through my head in staccato. Things like; Native Americans are stereotypically thought to have alcohol problems. Were these guys drunk?

Things like; I'd heard that the Apaches don't generally like white folks. Are these guys fucking with me on purpose? If I'm not ejected and thrown a thousand feet over a cliff, will I have to jump out of this truck and run? And worse, I'd heard there were Indian gangs to watch out for in these areas. These guys looked normal to me. What does an Apache gangster look like? Zoot suit and a ponytail?

All these paranoid thoughts of modern America had crept back into my head, the kind of ill-conceived thought I enjoyed being away from in my little oasis. The superfluous nonsense I was now full to the brim with after this trip and was increasingly anxious to get back to the oasis and once again, peacefully ignore.

There were ten solid minutes of this tumble down the mountain. After great concerted effort I was finally able to grab hold and get a permanent grip on the tailgate with my outstretched legs keeping me pressed against the sides.

A very harrowing experience to say the least.
I was a bit "spun-up" when the truck finally stopped.
The truck slowed and soon took a right turn onto a dirt road pulling into a parking area there at the turn. I was correct, this was the turn to Cibeque. No White folks allowed past this point. They are able to say that because this area is not the United States, this is the Apache Nation. I know these rules from previous experience and realized at that point I was at their whim. Generally speaking, white folks only get out of their cars and walk around on Indian reservations in the West when getting gas. Sometimes there are signs on the roads spelling out the restrictions. Was I about to get a terrible lesson in Native American relations? Should I have waited and stood hitching at the gas station there in Show Low until finding one long ride through the reservation?
When the truck stopped, within two seconds I threw my walking stick out of the truck bed, unsnapped and wriggled out of my pack and jumped out of the truck yanking my pack behind me. The truck doors flew open and the two speedsters jumped out laughing and hooting.

> *"Maaan that was a ride wasn't it! You good? didn't get banged up too much did you?"*

They were completely jovial and not at all menacing. It turned out one of my paranoid, rat-trapped thoughts was half correct. They explained to me that it *was* a "game" of sorts, they played it with their friends too.

They thought it would be fun to introduce an unwitting newcomer to a little Indian fun and thought I looked like I could handle it. I could feel the look on my face was saying "what the fuck?!" and as acceptance and relief washed over me, all I could say was,

"Can I go again? I think I have the grip down now."

This brought laughter from all three of us and soon we were talking about all kinds of things. They were proud White Mountain Apache Indians and wanted to know if I'd ever met a real Apache before. I told them yes, but not a White Mountain Apache. My oasis is next to the San Carlos Apache tribe reservation and the Apaches from there were often in the nearest town, Globe. I had also studied the plight of the Chiricahua Apache while I was living in Tombstone which instilled in me a sad reverence for Native Americans. Native American history with white people is a sad shame to us all.
I liked these two guys, they reminded me of me.
Staring at the "Cibeque" sign there on the dirt road I started wondering if I could somehow weedle my way down there and see what was forbidden a person of my skin color to see. Thinking this way I realized that standing at the doors of Cibeque, tables had been turned. I might as well have been a little black girl in Mississippi trying to go to an all white school. It's funny how these little epiphanies will find us if we are open to being found.

Before these two spirit teachers left down the forbidden road, I took their picture and they told me a White Mountain Apache secret.

> *"See that sign on the highway over there? There is a trail at that sign that goes to the tree line 40 feet away. Right at the tree line there is a chair in front of a tree. Sit in that chair, and the next Apache that comes bye going south will stop and pick you up."*

"Really? even if I'm not Indian?"

> *"Yes, it doesn't matter. If you know of the chair, an Indian must have told you. They'll think you're OK."*

Deal and done.
I sat in that cobbled up, make shift chair no more than three minutes before another truck pulled out of the dirt road heading South. The driver slowed to look at the chair, the truck stopped, and the passenger up front waved me in to... *the bed* of the truck again. This was actually the same model pickup truck as the last but with four doors. Inside was full with eight family members including Grandma and kids. At least this truck had a spray on bed liner to help keep me from sliding around. It was good that I had previously learned the riding position and grip because this guy gave no thought to me in the back of the truck as he careened through the winding downhill roads of the Salt River Canyon. He wasn't playing the game, he was just plain hauling ass.

Thirty minutes later at the gas station in Globe, I got out with a wave and a "Thanks!" expecting light conversation. The driver smiled, waved and turned away… that's all.

Wow, what a great native transportation system they've got going there.

It was six in the evening and darkness would be here in an hour or so. I could be a weenie and call someone at the oasis to come pick me up or I could stick it out and walk in like a conquering hero.

I chose the hero routine of course, what else?

It was still about twenty miles to the finish line so after a little rest and some eats I walked a mile or so to the corner of the highway that would take me home. That "T" intersection is surrounded by two sides of wasteland and one side of an off-road motorcycle and ATV playground park. By the time I got there, dusk was near so I resigned to one last night outdoors. It was a nice night and the playground area had a number of covered picnic tables. I picked the one furthest from the road and set up my gear for the last time. It turned out I wasn't the only one with this idea. By ten o'clock that night, there were three or four others in their vehicles who had come to rest.

I didn't sleep all that well on a picnic table with folks around but a couple hours was enough. When I woke, the previous nights visitors were already gone and by 6am new visitors had begun to arrive with their trucks and toys to use the park.

I got my gear together and pulled out the last piece of cardboard I'd saved.
Realizing this would be the last sign on my summer road trip I started to feel a romantic twinge for the road. I needed a sign that conveyed this to the passing public.
I stuck, "JUST A FEW MORE MILES" onto the back of my pack, lifted the pack over my shoulder, fastened it to me while walking, and headed out of the park.
I could see a small car sitting sideways in the front parking area next to the road. Most likely checking maps and distances before heading down this hundred-mile road to Tucson. I jokingly thought to myself, *"Aah, my limo has arrived."*
As I walked past the car I could see the older guy inside was wearing a dilby (*14) and was indeed looking down at a map. I thought about accosting him for my last ride but quickly stopped myself. I really didn't mind if I got a ride or not. I hadn't directly confronted anyone for a ride on this trip yet and now would be a terrible time to start. Besides, these last eighteen miles could be my swan song for the road, I didn't mind walking.
I strolled past the car without him looking up. By appearance alone, he looked to be the type that would consider picking me up. If that were the case, here I am, sign on my back, walking. About a hundred feet later I found it *was* the case.
Frank rolled up silently beside me in his Hybrid Toyota

and asked if I wanted a lift. He was traveling around, going places on the cheap and visiting a few old friends before moving permanently to a small town in Colorado. At this moment he was heading to Bisbee, Arizona to visit that cool little hippie town on the Mexican border one last time. There was a lot of stuff piled up in the car with one rear seat folded down to accommodate his sleeping bag. He called his car an NUV, "Nest Utility Vehicle." A nice twist on the boring, over-used vehicular acronym "SUV."

Frank turned out to be a pretty cool hipster type and was intrigued by my trip. He was elated when I told him he had the dubious honor of being my last ride. So much so that I invited him to breakfast at the oasis, it seemed fitting.

I'd really planned on walking the last two and a half miles on our dirt road alone. I imagined the last leg of my trip to be solitary and introspective. Forlorn music lightly playing on the breeze, romantically I'd be left by my final ride where the highway and our dirt road meet. No matter the time of day, I would walk the last miles in twilight of morning with a romanticized version of pomp and circumstance heard whisping across the desert. As I arrive, the gate would greet me by name and open wide to my gaze. There on the other side would be a packed kitchen on our weekly "spaghetti night" dinner or maybe on a Sunday morning for the "Waffle Brunch."

The traveling hero returns to a ticker tape parade basking in the glory of... yeah, whatever.
This was Sunday morning early, around seven, so when we got there and popped through the gate, nobody was up and around yet.
A quiet breakfast at a familiar table with Frank asking questions on the habits of our community was all it took. It was just the little bit of déjà vu I needed. This was what all visitors to our oasis end up doing, sitting around the table in wonder of the surroundings, asking questions. It was as though I'd never left, the perfect ending to my road trip. I had a fresh adventure under my belt to think back on fondly in the coming months and I was quickly back up to speed, back in the saddle.
Another epiphany struck me just then that took the past three months of travel to find me. The kind of thing that only happens after completing an arduous task, a growth spurt of conscience, a gift earned by toil. And it's so simple.
I realized why living in this little desert oasis in the middle of nowhere suits me,

...dirt roads have no curbs.

“Travel is fatal to prejudice, bigotry and narrow mindedness”

- *Mark Twain*

A Curb Caste Experience

Chapter Nine - Epilogue

Second Thoughts on the Road

I may have coined the phrase for the title of this book but the "Curb Caste" is an actual niche of society, a simpler level of humanity, a culture. It's a culture of basic human survival in a world where many struggle to endure. A culture in which many more dreams are dashed than are realized. A culture of dog-eat-dog, in-your-face without the rosy or misleading filters used by higher levels of society to mask nefarious ways. It's a culture of stark reality and the day-to-day struggle that implies.

We have many social sub-cultures in America, most of which are not showcased on our televisions and most of which exist at the curb level. American political policy follows the money and unfortunately many of the sub-cultures within America which drive our society are not based on money.

In todays United States, the "American Dream" is presented to us in many shiny ways, mainly to separate us from our money. The American Dream this country was founded on started out as one idea, and for one reason, Social Justice.

Unfortunately, somewhere along the way, Capitalism replaced social justice with money. Money is not an American dream, it's an American nightmare. Those without, generally live in "third world" conditions and eventually develop a type of third world mentality, displayed by their actions towards the world they live in. This would be evident if we could all just take a long walk across the United States.

While on this trip I journaled every night, which is how the outline of this book came to be. Along the way I also wrote down ideas, observations and realizations that came to me as I slogged open-mindedly through my journey. Acceptance is my mantra, but I am human, so a certain measure of judgment always comes first. Struggling with this judgment, many pithy and humorous ideas were explored such as...

- *Hitching while holding a sign on the street corner, thousands of faces pass me bye, all with different levels and means of avoidance. Nearly all are safely nurturing their worst hitch hiker fear, eyes cutting away from my gaze, double checking their locked car doors.*
  This gives me cause for a great daily affirmation...
  *... **I am not a Serial Killer**.*

- *Tourists go places to look and go home.*
  Travelers go places to engage and move on.

- *There is a definite line of demarcation on the roads between city garbage and country garbage. As a walking traveler, you can gauge how close you are to civilization* ***and*** *decide what you might like for your next meal when you get there, by the garbage along the road.*

- *Ego lives in the City and vacations to the country.*

- *Some never travel because they lack time or money. Some travel because they have time and money. Some people aspire to travel, waiting for the day when they will finally have time and money. Others travel because they have no money and plenty of time.*

- *When walking through the desert there is nothing better than cool water and a breeze across a sweat soaked shirt, and nothing more excruciating than the searing anticipation of shade from the next cloud.*

- *It is life affirming to be there at Sunrise to see light emerge from darkness. It gives anticipation for new beginnings to be there at Sundown as darkness temporarily replaces light. But even in the darkness, the moon and stars pierce the pitch as light, showing the way.*
  Light is always with us, darkness is temporary

- *From a hitch hiking standpoint, all surprises go better in long pants.*

- *At the bottom of a small ravine, I pick myself up and brush off after tripping on a protruding rock above and rolling down the hill. All I could think of was my mother often telling me as a child "pick up your feet!" She was concerned with the scraping sound of my dragging feet which annoyed her. Now, 45 years later I find the scraped elbows more concerning.*

- *How does the world work?*
  I'll bet Harvard or Princeton or Yale can sell us a key.
  Nah, The best education is travel.

- *I've never heard of anyone that doesn't like petrichor. The smell of the earth is hard to distinguish as we trip through our lives, mind pointed at trivial pursuits. But when it rains, in the country, the earth becomes a soup of our existence with a smell unequaled in olfactory memory, there can be no mistake. I rush outside when the rain starts. Blindly drawn to the smell, as a dogs nose is drawn to a cars open window. It's a chance to experience an occasional rarity. For me, it's a trigger for deep thought and meditation.*
  Poor, poor city folks.

- *Of all the different methods used to get a ride and move around the country, the one that was consistent in nurturing good conversation and got me the furthest, was to consistently and genuinely, smile.*

While walking, it was fun to imagine a trip like my own after thousands of people have done it. A lot of people are traveling around like this, so what's next? What kind of twist can we add to the routine to make it different?

I recently read about a guy who traveled to South America with only the clothes on his back. He depended on others for everything. I guess it turned out well, there were a lot of pictures of his journey, he has Very white teeth.

Hmm, I might make my next trip different by offering a tuna sandwich to everyone I meet. Or better yet, the diet on my next trip will consist entirely of black beans wrapped in cabbage leaves chased with soda, a gas chamber concoction. My sign would be fair warning, "HAVE GAS money." That one would go better with a video. The whole hitch hiking traveler genre could turn into a Johnny Knoxville take-off. No kidding though, if I travel around like this again, I'll be strapped with unseen mini-digital cameras. I can see a future book perhaps having an interactive website. Hyperlinks in the text of the "e" book will take you to vids of the actual situation. From skunk scares to bean burritos in small cars, "On Location with *TRAVELER.*"

...that seems like an awful lot of work... maybe not.

When I lived in southern Arizona I had an acquaintance named Steve who made his living from the side of the road. He didn't sell fruits or vegetables at a stand or wave a sign for a strip mall peddler, he walked the road.

In all of the Mexican border states there are actually two border crossing check points. One is at the border itself and the other is on every northbound road, dirt roads included, roughly twenty five miles north of the actual Mexican border. This creates a twenty-five mile strip of land through these states which is a hot bed for the illegal activity that actually made it across the main border crossing. Many people that make these South to North journeys aren't aware of the second border crossing and as they travel North and see the signs declaring the next inspection point, get very nervous about what they have in their possession. From the first warning sign till the actual border stop is usually about a mile, and in this mile many things are thrown out of car windows in a paranoid hurry.

Steve goes from station to station walking these miles, picking up "trash" from the side of the road for the good of our environment... and his wallet. He finds a lot of trash, bagfulls. It is not unusual for him to fill two thirty-gallon trash bags as he walks the northbound side. He happily does this nearly everyday at different checkpoints but never crosses the checkpoint or even leaves the trash at the checkpoint dumpster. He takes the trash home and goes through it again because he puts everything in the bag. Soda cups and bags of pot, candy wrappers and bags of meth. Empty bottles and drug smoking pipes.

Fast food bags and open but nearly full liquor bottles. All kinds of contraband are found, including the occasional gun. His life is one big treasure hunt that never fails to please.

All along my trip I kept Steve in mind by keeping my eyes down. I didn't do nearly as well as Steve but I did OK for an amateur. I found a twenty dollar bill along the road in Louisiana, a small bag of meth in a bar parking lot in California (I traded it for pot), several pieces of jewelry and a lot of change. In one place, someone had stopped on the side of the road and hastily emptied their car ashtray on the ground. Normally, I wouldn't have picked through the pile of butts and ash but the wind had scattered it a bit revealing a man's wedding ring shining underneath. It caught my eye from twenty feet away.

So I guess the moral to this little snippet is that there are other benefits to being on the curb besides ultimate freedom and the occasional adventure.

One thing I noticed while hitching which amuses me now more than then, were the manners of avoidance. Something you must do when walking the road is to catch the eye of the driver. Whether you are crossing the street, hailing a cab or hitching a ride, your eyes and the drivers eyes must meet. When hitching, I'm gauging car movements and drivers attention as well as looking straight at them. It's actually mentally tiring after a few hours.

It becomes a staccato of faces and after a while you can tell the "hell-no," from the "excuse," to the "stop and pull over," from just the slightest eye movement or lip twitch. That's *if* you caught their eye.
Sometimes you know they saw you even if your eyes don't meet, by their actions.
There are always the folks that deadpan right past you stiff as a board pretending you aren't there. A variant of this is exactly the same but with a very short eye cut over and back. Or of course the same two in an over-relaxed posture. I had several people purposefully gun their motors precisely as they were passing me. The scarier minds did it before reaching me and a couple of them even gave a quick swerve of the wheel to give me a double pantload as they passed.
Some people were noticeably frightened and changed lanes or pulled further from the curb till past.
I often heard door locks clack as cars passed.
I think my favorite was the overt excuse.
People would look at me with a forlorn look and a shrug, often mouthing an apology. Sometimes they would measure a distance between their thumb and index finger. This of course was to show me they are only going a short distance but it was more fun to imagine them telling me, *"my dick's only this big."* I would wave to them and shout *"SORRY!!"* as they glanced back at me in the rearview.

A few people tried giving me money as I stood there holding a sign hitching.

This older guy pulled up close to the curb and reached over to the passenger side window to push a dollar bill through an 1/8"crack he'd opened it to. Despite his honest intent, the wadded up bill wouldn't be pushed through the crack. The cars piled up behind him as I tried to tell him I'd take a ride instead. The bill, the window and the honking frustrated him enough that he left in a huff, cussing a blue streak. It was a bit disheartening, I felt sorry for that.

I was a little surprised when folks offered me money. It happened several times and I declined each time. In fact, when I was in Goletta, California talking with my fishy panhandler friend in front of the McYuckys, an older couple came out of the restaurant and made a scene about giving both of us a dollar. It was like an old silent movie. With overly dramatic gestures and facial expressions, the gentleman made a production of digging his money out and going through it. He then handed us each a dollar bill, not a word was said. Their facial expressions told the whole story. Fishy was first, staring at the man's hands greedily like a dog might stare at cheese he knows he will soon get a piece of. When he offered me my dollar bill, I held up my hand in refusal but his brow furrowed and he shook the bill gently at me insisting. I tried to explain but he had gone too far and had to be rid of the bill, so I took it from him and gave it to Fishy. You'd think I had slapped his wife by the look the old guy gave me. He really got ticked.

Imagine my gall, giving a panhandler the dollar meant for me.
After the incidents of me turning down money, four times according to my journal, I started to think that perhaps I should graciously take it. It can only be a good deed and make the giver feel as though they are helping if I did. And what did it say about me and my idea of the homeless? I didn't want to be mistaken for a panhandler for the cost of a dollar? After thinking about it and deciding I would no longer refuse, people stopped offering.
Lesson learned.

A subject that always arises when talking about hitch hiking or foot travel is safety and security. Many people thought I was nuts not taking a small gun with me. Especially considering my previous encounter that landed me in the hospital. To this I sometimes relay a core lesson of violent conflict.
The victim is never ready for what's coming.
No matter how much we prepare, its seldom enough. Aggressors don't file letters of intent and many times they don't pick out their victim in advance. For me and the realizations I have come upon, the safest and most secure thing a person can do is to be honest, nice, and smiley. This type of attitude is infectious and de-escalates most situations without violence. My entire trip was a testament to this practice. Positive motion begets positivity.

The other circumstances that occur beyond our control are best dealt with by using a good pair of shoes. Besides, I did have a security blanket of sorts with me. A friend of mine in Southern Arizona was worried for me on my trip and also wanted pictures via phone of places I visited. I put Debbie's number on speed dial, just in case, and zipped off pics to her on occasion. Knowing there was someone I know in my pocket other than beleaguered police officers at the end of a 911 call was a comfort. I guess it's just nice to know someone is personally interested and that there was moral support at the ready.
That's a different kind of security isn't it? We should all try it. It feels better than packing a gun.
Thank You Debbie.

I am often told how traveling and living the life I lead is easy now that I receive a monthly disability stipend. I would agree with that, but for far different reasons than the casual observer might realize. I feel that being in the position I am now in, and living the way I do, realizes the actual freedom that most of us look for. I have very few wants, and my basic minimum needs are met. No payments no encumbrance, and because of this, the costs in my life are very little in comparison to most Americans. Isn't this the "no worries" and "free from debt" type of situation many of us really aspire to? At one time I was well off, and as hard as I tried, money never bought me freedom. All money did was to create a need for more money and the endless struggle to acquire even more and protect what I already had. It's the lack of money and being able to clear my mind of the struggle for money that got me to this place. At one time, long ago, American life was about throwing off our chains of monetary control, now those thoughts are all but forgotten.

My American dream doesn't include taking from someone else. It doesn't include payments or long hours of overtime to buy the next shiny item presented. From my position I can see how everyone could live in the same manner as myself, but of course having been in the same position many are, I can also understand why they don't.

To have an adventure of any sort we can't be sitting still waiting for it to come to us. We must shut off the TV and leave our house. Experiences like the ones in this book don't come to your town and find you. They aren't standing there on your stoop when you open the door. You have to get out in the mix, put yourself out there, meet people, go places... do things out of your comfort zone... live.

I myself am normally a bit of a recluse. I enjoy my own company and am comfortable in my own head.

In everyday life I don't have much to say, who's really listening anyway?

Hitch hiking is a completely different story. If someone stopped to pick me up, it was generally as company for themselves rather than a ride for me. I'd say about eighty percent of the time, folks who stopped to pick me up just needed someone on which to unload their pent up jabber. Many didn't care if I was listening or not. Several people talked non-stop without a break, others would speak over my replies. Maybe they just didn't want to be seen driving down the road talking to themselves, I don't know. Whatever the reason, I was forced to engage, and also for whatever reason, it was OK with me.

We could all take a tip from my White Mountain Apache friends. It would be great if somehow a large percentage of us were to put our cars aside and commute alternatively. The bus, train, carpool, bicycle, etc. is far better for humanity and the earth all the way around. We experience more of our world and generally save quite a bit of money. We meet more people, lower pollution, give less money to corporate oil and auto manufacturing... the list goes on.
This is the way things change, one of us at time. Soon a few more people will take notice, and before you know it, the thoughts running through our heads become a thing.
Come on, lets start a thing.

If ideas such as these are too much for your lifestyle, that's completely understandable in todays bustling world, but still, there is one small thing you can do... live vicariously, give somebody a ride. ☺

The End

Reference Index

*1 – **Car Sick** by John Waters – Macmillan Press - 2014

*2 – **Rod Serling** – Writer and narrator of the TV series' "The Twilight Zone" and "Night Stalker" From the 1960's/70's

*3 - **Rocky Horror Picture Show** – Jim Sharman/ 20th Century Fox – 1975

*4 – **Cholo** – Slang - a Latin American with Indian blood; a mestizo. a lower-class Mexican, especially in an urban area. A teenage boy, especially in a Mexican-American community, who is a member of a street gang.

*5 – **"The Worlds Most interesting Man"** is a Dos Equis Beer advertising meme where the tag line *"I don't always drink beer, but when I do, it's Dos Equis"* has been morphed into many humorous twists.

*6 – **Even Cowgirls get the blues** – Gus Van Sant/ New Line Cinema - 1993

*7 **– Jeremiah Johnson** – Sydney Pollack / Warner Brothers Pictures - 1973

*8 - **Grizzly Adams** - a TV series in 1977-78 featuring a grizzled outdoor mountain man.

*9 – **PDQ** – Pretty Damn Quick – mid west vernacular

*10 – **M. Night Shyamalan** is a Writer/Director of horror, thriller movies such as "The sixrth Sense", "Signs" and "The Village"

*11 – **"Babs and Newman"** are two characters on the television situation comedy "Seinfeld" played by Sheree North and Wayne Knight. When they meet, their banter turns to that of an old black an white movie such as "The Maltese Falcon".

*12 – **Thelma and Louise** – Ridley Scott/ Pathe' Entertainment - 1991

*13 – **Sweeny Todd** is a fictional character as the villain in the Victorian Penny Dreadful "The String of Pearls" from 1846. He was a revengeful barber that slit his clients throats while in the chair, dumping them in a chute to the kitchen of the meat pie shop below his Barber shop. In 2007, Tim Burton Directed the movie "Sweeny Todd" starring Johnny Depp.

*14 – **Dilby** is a type of mans hat similar to a fedora but with a very narrow brim. This old style hat has become popular with the hipster crowd.

Look for other Interesting Books
by Michael McNaney
on Amazon and Kindle,
- or –
better yet, ask for them at
Your Favorite Book Store

Made in the USA
Columbia, SC
04 October 2020